Separa

Separate and Dominate

Feminism and Racism After the War on Terror

BY

CHRISTINE DELPHY

Translated by David Broder

VERSO

London • New York

This English-language edition published by Verso 2015
Translation © David Broder 2015
First published as *Classer, dominer: Qui sont les autres?*
© La Fabrique 2008

Chapter 2 was prepared for a hearing of the Parity Commission,
presented in front of Gisèle Halimi and Roselyne Bachelot, 14 May 1996;
Chapter 7 was presented on behalf of the Collectif féministe pour l'égalité
at the meeting 'Une école pour toutes et pour tous' [A School for All],
4 February 2004; Chapter 8 was a contribution to the
Actuel Marx conference, September 2004.

Author and publisher would like to acknowledge the publication
of earlier versions of the following: Chapter 3, *Politique la revue*, June 1997;
Chapter 4, written together with Jacques Bidet, Danièle Kergoat, Willy Pelletier,
and Jacques Texier, *L'Humanité*, 23 October 2001; Chapter 5, *Contretemps*,
March 2002; Chapter 6, *Nouvelles Questions féministes*, 21 January 2002;
Chapter 8, Jacques Bidet (ed.), *Guerre impériale, guerre sociale*, Paris:
PUF, 2005; Chapter 9, *Assises de l'anticolonialisme postcolonial*, 2005;
Chapter 10, *Nouvelles Questions féministes*, 25 January 2006.

1 3 5 7 9 10 8 6 4 2

Verso
UK: 6 Meard Street, London W1F 0EG
US: 20 Jay Street, Suite 1010, Brooklyn, NY11201
www.versobooks.com

Verso is the imprint of New Left Books

ISBN-13: 978-1-78168-880-9 (PB)
ISBN-13: 978-1-78168-879-3 (HB)
eISBN-13: 978-1-78168-881-6 (US)
eISBN-13: 978-1-78168-882-3 (UK)

British Library Cataloguing in Publication Data
A catalogue record for this book is available from the British Library

Library of Congress Cataloging-in-Publication Data
A catalog record for this book is available from the Library of Congress

Typeset in Monotype Sabon by Hewer Text Ltd, Edinburgh
Printed in the US by Maple Press

Contents

Introduction to the English-Language Edition

This book deals with the oppression of all people we commonly call 'Others'. These include women, queer people, Guantánamo inmates, civilians bombed in Afghanistan by the forces of civilization, and 'Arab' women excluded from school by the same forces in France. Despite the varied ways these groups experience oppression, their oppression also appears to share certain traits in common, if examined through the theoretical lens of the 'Other'. Societies deploy certain mechanisms in order to fabricate Others, and I argue that the discourse on the Other is above all a justification of the non-discursive fact that Others live under the thumb of the 'Ones'. Nobody talks about the Ones even though it is self-evident – or should be – that the One and the Other go together like a horse and carriage.

Every country, every society has its own Others, and the ones I discuss here are for the most part French. But only for the most part. All Western societies share Others in common: women, queer people, vulnerable foreign civilians. Even the Guantánamo inmates are our common responsibility – as a consequence of the 'Allied' in War on Terror.

Different societies use different mechanisms to frame some as Ones and some as Others. The mechanisms are material: they are about denying them equality and treating them as not quite up to the mark, abnormal, or downright sub-human. Instilling in them these beliefs about themselves, depriving them of self-confidence, of a sense of their worth, of dignity, of the conviction that such a thing as justice exists. Making them doubt themselves and the world is both a result of their concrete, material oppression, and a means to prevent them from fighting it.[1]

I began writing these chapters in 1996. Are the situations I describe outdated? I wish they were, but they are not. The established Ones remain resilient. The political scene is solidly occupied by White men who give no sign of wanting to give up their positions. In France, conservative parties are ready to forego huge state subsidies in order not to have to present a number of women candidates on their party lists equal to the number of men there. And what is true of the rather rich middle-aged conservative men is also true of the young, poor, leftist men, who are not ready to let women talk at meetings, to let them get a word in about what the society of the future should look like.

In France, for the last forty years, there has been talk of fighting racial discrimination, but no measures whatsoever have been taken to that end.

At the same time as Europe was urging all its members to fight discrimination, there emerged a notion that Islam was the problem. And the Ones, including members of the ultra-left, agreed. Islam had not been a problem so far. But some teenage girls started going to high school wearing headscarves. And, gradually, between 1989 and 2003, this was constructed by anti-Arab lobbies as an act contrary to the French version of political

---

1 And of course they are not in any way different. Hierarchy is not created by arranging pre-existing categories of people; quite the opposite. This is what I wrote in 1989 about sex and gender: gender – the hierarchy, precedes sex. The emphasis put on 'genital difference' is but the marker of hierarchical order. First published in French in 1991, in English in 1993: 'Rethinking Sex and Gender', *Women's Studies International Forum* 16/1, Jan.–Feb. 1993, republished in *L'ennemi principal*, Paris: Syllepse, 1989–2013.

secularism, *laïcité*.[2] Gradually, the children and grandchildren of immigrants from North Africa, a territory recently vacated by the French, who had conquered and occupied it for one hundred and thirty years, children and grandchildren born in France and French, started to be called 'second- (or third-)generation immigrants'. Not French. Immigrants. Gradually they were perceived as and called 'Muslims'.

Political secularism was deemed to be under threat, endangered by this Other religion (which many descendants of immigrants do not practise). For forty years, hardly a week went by without one or other of France's two main weeklies (*L'Express* and *Le Point*) showing a fully veiled woman on its front cover with a caption along the lines of 'Is Islam compatible with democracy?'[3] This attack on a culture – for even to the non-practising, Islam was the religion of their family, was part of their roots – led a part of the younger generation to embrace it anew, thus confirming the worst suspicions of the 'true French' (the Whites).

After years of being both brainwashed and confirmed in their racism and their dominant status (the one thing that really matters), the Whites, who had never socialized with Arabs or with the black part of the population, who had relegated non-White communities to the outskirts of cities and towns, who kept for themselves the best housing, the best schools, the best jobs – and in the last thirty years the few jobs – had found a 'good reason' to go on discriminating: 'these people' are just not deserving of equal opportunities.

And so things have been going from bad to worse. These home-grown rationalizations of racism find significant

<hr>

2   Saïd Bouamama, *L'affaire du foulard islamique, la production d'un racisme respectable*, Paris: Le Geai bleu, 2004.

3   Thomas Deltombe, *L'islam imaginaire, La construction médiatique de l'islamophobie en France, 1975–2005*, Paris: La Découverte, 2005.

support in the international arena. People of Arab descent identify – how could they not? – with Palestinians, and get angry about French support for brutal Israeli policies: the regular massacres of Gazan civilians, the annexation and colonization of Palestinian land, not to mention their constant harassment by Israeli 'settlers'. This identification is deemed criminal by the Establishment.

To that one must add the fact that for the last twenty years, the Middle East has been the target of military attacks and invasions, which have left it in utter chaos. And for what? The reason for these Western wars – in which France has participated, with the exception of the last war in Iraq – is still waiting to be discovered by historians not yet born. Anti-Muslim, anti-Arab propaganda is not waning. On the contrary. In the fall of 2014 a book-length pamphlet prophesying the replacement of the French population by Muslims became an instant bestseller in France.[4] The author, in an interview given to an Italian newspaper, said French Muslims ought to be deported (to where, he didn't say).

France was the *only* country in the world to prohibit marches denouncing the Bombing of Gaza in the summer of 2014. Can one be surprised that some 'third-generation immigrants' – in fact an amazingly small number of them – incensed at the way they are treated by their own country (France) – run amok?

With the recent assassination by Muslim youths of twelve people working for the 'satirical' journal *Charlie Hebdo* – which consistently derided and insulted Islam – and four customers in a Jewish supermarket, things got far worse. There was a downward plunge, and the prime minister announced that France was now at war. He did not say with whom, but it was clear to everybody that the enemy was inside our walls.

The French state is not willing to take any responsibility for

---

4   Eric Zemmour, *Le Suicide français*, Paris: Albin Michel, 2014.

what has happened, and will happen again. It has created the conditions for a civil war, of low intensity but a civil war nonetheless. Women wearing a headscarf are little by little being excluded from jobs in the public sector, and now in the private sector as well – in the name of their emancipation. As parents, they are now forbidden from accompanying their children on school outings. This persecution is disguised as the defence of French secularism (*laïcité*).

For in the last fifteen years the meaning of that word has been changed, so that it now means a prohibition against expressing one's faith in public. The current president, François Hollande, even said in his speech on the day he was elected that religion belonged to the private, even 'intimate', realm. This is in sharp contradiction with the French law of 1905, which instituted political secularism – *laïcité* – by decreeing the separation of church and state, with the aims and spirit of that law. The same law guarantees freedom of conscience and the freedom to follow whatever belief one chooses. International conventions – be it the Universal Declaration of Human Rights or the European Convention of Human Rights – guarantee freedom of conscience and of speech *in public* and in private. Laïcité was never mentioned by anyone before the 2004 law banning headscarves in state schools. But the European Court of Justice (ECJ), created to enforce the European Convention, is not doing its job. Its rulings in the few cases brought by Muslim parents protesting their daughters' exclusion from school are contradictory. On the one hand, the French defence is that banning the headscarf in state schools strengthens the value of *vivre ensemble*[5] (a notion that does not appear in

---

5   *Vivre ensemble* (living together) is the buzzword in discussions of race and ethnicity in France. It implies a defence of the status quo, in other words living together without changing anyone's situation or status in society – you in your place, me in mine.

any law); the ECJ finds this concept vague and unexplained, and does not see how this ban will contribute to social cohesion. But, on the other hand, in its ruling the ECJ accepts this weak argument, stating that each European country's 'traditions' must be respected – and obviously take precedence over fundamental rights. It takes the weak notion of *vivre ensemble* as being part of French *laïcité*, to which it gives the status of one of these national traditions. But the ECJ upholds the French state's use of *laïcité* to justify discrimination. Furthermore, in 2004 most feminists, unfortunately, sided with the government and approved the school headscarf ban.

And for the last fifteen years, this defective and faulty, or rather falsified, definition of political secularism has become the prevailing belief of the majority of the population.[6] Part of this population – the Left – is still living the anti-papist fight of a hundred years ago, and equates secularism with atheism, and although it does not openly say it, would like to make all religions illegal. However, even these extremists (*laïcards*) never protest the fact that the state pays for the upkeep of 36,000 churches, among other official marks of indulgence for the Christian faith. Nor are very many seen rising up against the fact that political secularism is not applied in five *départements* of France, where priests, pastors and rabbis are paid by the state just as they were under Napoleon. Yet, at the same time as they want to make the state school a 'sanctuary', they never mention that almost half of all French children and teenagers are educated in religious-run (mostly Catholic) schools.

Two weeks after the January 7 killings, the French government presented a plan aimed at reducing the risks of further attacks and putting the onus on schools. More

---

6   Jean Baubérot, *La laïcité falsifiée*, Paris: La découverte, 2012.

courses on republican values are to be taught, and the French *laïcité* – which in practice means obliging Muslims, and Muslims alone, to make themselves invisible – has pride of place in that plan. The words 'Republic' and 'Republican values' are quoted in this document twenty-five times, whereas 'equality' appears only once, and discrimination not at all.

A week after the murders, numerous large marches took place; the most popular slogan was 'Je Suis Charlie'. Another slogan often repeated was 'Freedom of speech'. Throughout the media, the journalists who had been killed were mourned and eulogized as martyrs who died in support of 'Freedom of speech', which thus became, in the words of journalists, the jewel in the crown of the French republic. This reading implied that the dead men had criticized all religions equally; but in fact they had reserved their most frequent and vicious attacks for Islam. None of the media bothered to mention that Islam is the religion or the culture of the most underprivileged and loathed people in France, regularly denounced by not-at-all subversive dailies and weeklies, and that it does not take much anti-conformism and even less courage to draw cartoons packed with racist jokes that Muslims – and Arab-looking people more generally – must suffer in silence every day of their lives.

Freedom of speech does not have the iconic, self-defining status in France it enjoys in the US. The reality is in fact altogether different. Several laws limit it severely. In particular the 'Gayssot law' makes it a crime to raise questions about the Holocaust. Even research into the Holocaust has become next to impossible.

There was a very clear example of the perverse double talk emanating from the state a few days later. The minister for education asked teachers to organize debates about the killings in schools. Less than a week later she expostulated that she was extremely shocked by what she had learnt about these debates. She said there had been 'incidents' during the minute of silence that had been called for.[7] She said, 'Even where there have been no incidents, there was too much questioning from students like: "I am Charlie, but . . . why is there a double standard: why defend freedom of speech here and not there?" *These questions are unbearable.*'[8] To the minister, these sessions were meant to tell the children the official truth about the events, never to actually discuss them.

Fortunately about a week later, two women teachers took issue with this view of education, observing that their pupils' questions, as 'unbearable' as they had been deemed by the minister, were pertinent and that they had had interesting and rational debates with their charges. Meanwhile children as young as eight years old are being taken to police stations for having refused to say 'Je Suis Charlie', after being asked three times by their teacher to do so.[9] However, the minister's outburst did not put a lid on the issue as she had obviously hoped. Gradually the truth about the journalists who were shot is being aired. Essayists and commentators write or say on TV that while we can be – and should be – horrified that these men were killed, we can nonetheless acknowledge that they were producing a sexist and racist journal. Some go as far as to say, like their British and American counterparts, that freedom implies responsibility: that even if the law allows it, you can, and must, refrain from gravely offending people. And some ask the same 'unbearable' questions as the children: why is the same

---

7 Some of which were denounced to the police.

8 Lepoint.fr, 'Attentats: Vallaud-Belkacem recense 200 incidents dans les écoles', 14 January 2015.

9 Liberation.fr, 'Un enfant de 8 ans au commissariat pour "apologie du terrorisme" ', 28 January 2015.

sentence a 'joke', an expression of free speech in one case, and an 'apologia for terrorism'[10] in another case?[11]

However, the same treatment is not meted out to adults with social status. The double standard reveals to those who never suspected its existence the ugly authoritarian streak in French culture. Meanwhile the government wants to maintain the spirit of January 11 (the big marches): 'national unity'. But the unity of the nation is, here as elsewhere, an ideology disguising the fact that said nation is divided along gender lines, ethnic lines, class lines, into Haves and Have-nots, of course, but also into Speak and Speak-not: into Ones and Others.

Christine Delphy, February 2015

---

10 A deed without any clear definition, made into a penal offence by the latest anti-terrorist law.

11 Lately one man has been sentenced to two years in jail, the only evidence against him being the testimony of another man who had – or so he said – heard him express support for the murderers in a food store. Another (who was drunk on a bus at night) has been sentenced to four years for the same 'offence'.

CHAPTER I

Who's Behind the 'Others'?

The texts in this book have one objective in common. That is, to elaborate a materialist approach to not only oppression and marginalization, but also domination and normality. These themes are pairs of opposites; we can't have the one without the other. Some will say that we've heard all this before. But it is a lesson that has not been widely received. So here I am insisting on what I have been repeating over the years, principally as regards the opposition between women and men: this division is constructed at the same time as the hierarchy between them, and not before. It is at the same moment, in the same movement, that a division or distinction is both created and created as a hierarchy, opposing the superior to the inferior.

As I have already written elsewhere,[1] this is a theory of the divisions produced in society. These divisions are both dichotomous and comprehensive. If you are not in one group, you are in the other.

The other – and even the Other, with a capital O – is often invoked as an explanation of the phenomena that I'm addressing here: the oppression of women, of non-whites and of gays. In this view, in order to put an end to discrimination based on gender, race and sexuality, it is necessary – and sufficient – to decide once and for all to 'accept the Other'.

Indeed, we often hear, in newspaper columns or in the

---

1 *L'ennemi principal*, Vol. I, 'Économie politique du patriarcat', Paris: Syllepse, 1999.

writings of philosophers, sociologists and other scholars, that the hierarchy in our society is due to the 'rejection of the Other'. Except when it comes to the opposition between 'capitalists' and 'workers'. That is not to say that there was never a time when that question, too, was treated like this: but a hundred and fifty years ago Marxism replaced this with a materialist analysis.

Since 1975, when I wrote 'Pour un féminisme matérialiste',[2] I have opposed all idealist 'explanations' of the oppression of women, instead advancing a materialist approach. And the thesis that claims that human beings cannot stand 'difference' is a thesis on human nature: an essentialist thesis and, therefore, an idealist one. This approach does not only apply to the oppression of women; and here I also present texts dealing with the oppression of non-whites and of gays.

What these three oppressions have in common is that each of them divides the whole of society, the whole population, into two categories, into two camps. But each of them sets its own line of separation, dividing the same population with which we started – let's say, the population living on French territory – in a different manner. Since there is a different principle behind each of these three divisions, the dominant and dominated groups that these principles constitute are different in each of the three cases. But since we're always beginning from the same population, and given that each of these divisions is exhaustive, each of these dominant and dominated groups is in turn dissected by the second and then the third principle of division. So a person could be in the dominant group according to one division and the dominated group according to another, and then again belong to the dominant group according to the third division; or be

---

2 Pour un féminisme matérialiste', *L'Arc*, April 1975. Republished in *L'ennemi principal*, Vol. I.

dominant in all three cases, or always in the dominated group.

The end result of these processes is that each person is necessarily defined as a woman or a man, a non-white or a white, a homosexual or a heterosexual.

The articulation, imbrication or interlinking of these different oppressions, and the set of combinations resulting from their criss-crossing, are one of the main focuses of sociology and in particular of feminist sociology. But they are not the object of this collection. In bringing together texts devoted to oppressions based on gender, race and sexuality, what I want to emphasize is the similarity among the operations that give priority to one group and stigmatize another.

I also want to show not only that the problematic of the Other fails to explain sexism, racism, homophobia, or any other social hierarchy, but that it presupposes the existence of such hierarchies.

The object of this collection, then, is principally to show that hatred of 'the different' is not a 'natural' trait of the human species. I do so firstly by examining the arbitrary fashion in which the Western tradition – formalized in philosophy – has posed this hatred as a universal, constituent element of the human psyche and invented the concept of the 'Other'. Secondly, I show that this other is socially constructed through concrete material practices, including ideological and discursive ones – it does not express some hypothetical 'human nature', which is an ideological concept.

These texts share the same problematic, but they differ in their very varied style and format, which reflect the diversity of the circumstances in which they were produced. Some were academic papers for conferences or journals, while others were interventions in political meetings, articles for newspapers, or submissions to government committee hearings.

The concept of the Other as an invention of the Western tradition

There are two reasons why 'hatred of the different' cannot explain the existence of stigmatized groups in our societies.

The first is that an explanation in terms of 'rejection of the other' is a psychologizing approach; that is, it transposes theories based on the individual psyche onto the plane of phenomena regarding how societies function.

The second is that this psychology – this theory of the individual psyche – is itself part of a particular, Western philosophy that addresses the question of the 'other person' from the viewpoint of the 'I'. Let's begin with this second reason.

I. Even to describe the question in the manner that Western philosophy has historically addressed it immediately brings the 'I' to the fore. When I speak of philosophy, I mean the invisible, subterranean foundations of the worldview [*Weltanschauung*] that a culture shares in common.[3] With that caveat, we can say that ever since Plato, the Western worldview – as it's been expressed by the people credited with revealing these foundations, the 'philosophers' – is firstly a reflection on the self, and after that a reflection on the world. However, philosophy does recognize the world's existence, and it is thus

---

3 Indeed it would be mistaken to consider philosophy – as a discipline or as a corpus of texts – as if it were *sui generis*, and still less as if it guided 'ordinary people's' worldview. It is obvious enough that these people have not read the philosophers' works. These philosophers are expressing this jointly held view, nothing more – it's just that they explicate it. And as 'sages', in formalizing this worldview they in turn influence it. But when I cite certain authors, this is justified insofar as their formulations exemplify presuppositions that inform the Western worldview; and not by some wish to take a side in any of the debates internal to philosophy in the strict sense, as a discipline (for example the so-called theories 'of the subject' and the responses to them) and still less in the competition among disciplines.

fully justified in examining what viewpoint it assumes as its basis for looking out at the world – this viewpoint being the 'I'. But in this philosophy, the 'I' is alone. All by itself and constitutive. It does not pose the question of the other person, because this other person is not necessary but superfluous. The 'I' embodies consciousness, and if there is one human consciousness that can see the world and see itself seeing it, there is no need for any other consciousness. This first, singular consciousness – the only necessary one – tells us 'I think therefore I am' (Descartes) but never asks what the conditions of possibility of its thinking are.

For example, notwithstanding Descartes's hilarious description of his childhood in his first *Meditation*, he seems never to have been brought into the world or brought up; language came to him just like that, and he learnt to write without anyone teaching him – and we don't know why he wrote, because he was apparently not writing for anyone. He was perfectly indifferent to the conditions of possibility for his existence and of him sitting down one fine day to write '*Cogito ergo sum*' – and he wasn't hungry or thirsty or cold – some invisible entities took care of that – he didn't give them half a thought. More than one academic's wife will recognize her husband in this portrait . . . So it is a philosophy of the dominant, for whom material life plays out to *their benefit* – the necessities of their survival are fulfilled, but *externally to them*. This disdain for the conditions of possibility of one's own existence and own thinking is taken yet further, with the denial of society as a whole. Well, no individual can exist outside of society. There can be no human without a society, and no thought without language; the very existence of individuals indispensably depends on there being some collectivity, even if it is just a few dozen people. The very notion of the individual is linguistic, and therefore social. The hyperindividualism of Western philosophy borders on solipsism and autism. It cannot provide the foundation for a psychology worthy of the name – which must take into account the conditions of possibility for not just this or that individual psyche, but the psyche as such.

And the notion of the Other as a pre-existing and, in short, 'natural' reality comes to us precisely from this erroneous psychology, one of the major constituent parts of Western philosophy. In all this Western tradition, formulated and then built up by the philosophers, it is in Hegel that the other person appears as a 'philosophical question' that we need to account for. Here, this other appears as a threat to the expression of the subject, as Sartre later remarked by adopting his famous formula: 'Each conscience seeks the death of the other.'

As such, Western philosophy, which claims to speak the truth about human beings independently of their time or place, without needing to specify their concrete situations in a given society, decrees that the 'other person' is dangerous. This philosophy tells us that its object – human beings in general – can only be alarmed by the existence of others, and if it were possible would gladly do without them. For the Western tradition, to think the human condition means thinking it on the basis of a human being who is alone on this Earth and would prefer things to stay that way.

This philosophy *is thus simultaneously a psychology*, because it describes or predicts reactions (of worry faced with the other person) and desires (of solitude). And as a psychology, this theory is not just solipsist: it's flat-out crazy. After all, as Francis Jacques writes in a brilliant synthesis, it ultimately ends up saying: 'If a being exists, what need is there for beings? If one exists, what need is there for many?'[4] It is

---

4 Francis Jacques, *Dialogiques, Recherches logiques sur le dialogue*, Paris: PUF, 1979.

crazy in that it denies the reality of the world of human beings (and, besides, of all living things) including the subject of the consciousness that it is discussing. Today orthodox psychoanalysis (Freud and Lacan) embodies the paradigmatic expression of this Western vision, this having become the basis not only of the psychology taught in French universities but also of the 'pop science' most widespread among the general public. It has arrived at the extreme limit of solipsism: posing the existence of an 'intra-psychic reality' that has nothing to do with what happens or has happened in individuals' lives.

II. But now we come to the first reason why explanations in terms of 'rejection of the Other' are inadequate. Indeed, whatever the validity of psychological theories on the plane on which they claim to operate (the functioning of the individual psyche), we can in no case use them as our basis for explaining how groups relate to one another.

After all, even if we were here dealing with a materialist psychology in which the other is always-already present in the consciousness of each person, in this passage from psychology to sociology there is an epistemologically unjustifiable change of scale.

Scientific sociology constantly runs into the psychologizing reductionism of spontaneous psychology, which tautologically explains police violence in terms of the brutality of policemen and domestic violence in terms of bad husbands. In reality, of course, it is the organization of society that not only makes individuals violent but also allows them to be violent – and not individual traits pre-existing society.

But why is spontaneous sociology founded on such a false, individualizing and essentialist vision, if not because this vision, which implies that the relations among people are not organized by society, is the very ideology of our society?

Scientific understanding recognizes the methodological

inadmissibility of transposing the level of individual consciousness onto the level of society, and of understanding groups and the relations among them as a large-scale reflection of mental processes proper to individuals or the relations among individuals. Society is not a big individual; it can be explained only in terms of social processes, which are not of the same order as psychological processes.

So even if our individual psychology were of the type described by Western philosophy, and even if this psychology dictated that each of us feared the 'other person', this would be of no help in explaining why entire groups see and name other entire groups as 'others'.

However, this is what happens when we are constantly exhorted – as individuals but also as a set of individuals, as a group called 'Us' – to 'accept the Other' and thus put an end to sexism, racism and homophobia.

The collective creation, the organization that is society, prevails over individuals and pre-exists each of them – because we are born to an already existing society. Society cannot however be conceived as a plus-size individual, nor as the sum of the individuals within it. It does need them – no society can survive without its members – and even more so, they need it, because a human being cannot be human, or even simply survive, outside of society. Yet this interdependence does not imply that these two phenomena have the same rules of functioning. Society is not an individual. Even if we can accept that each individual, confined within her own skin and her physiological and psychological functioning, perceives the other person as distinct from her – which certainly doesn't mean fearing and rejecting them! – the same cannot be said of society. Society cannot have a problem with the 'other' person, because it has no psyche: the expression 'collective consciousness' is a metaphor.

*

Who's Behind the 'Others'?

'The other par excellence is the feminine, through which a world behind the scenes extends the world.'
– Emmanuel Lévinas[5]

Which is something to think about for all those Others who imagine the 'Ones'[6] are messing around when they don't treat them as human beings. Let's go back to the exhortation to accept the Other, or 'otherness', or 'difference'. This Other is rather vague: it could mean other people who have the same God or humanism as me, even if it's not apparent at first sight. It could also be a whole bunch of others, and in general, it is that: it is a stigmatized group whose stigmatization goes unmentioned.

We think we understand, because we call them 'the Other' and because we know that we 'struggle to accept the other'. This discourse is such a commonplace that it is impossible to go a day without reading or hearing it, and yet it also contains something of a mystery. Everyone seems to know who these Others are; everyone talks about them, but they never speak.

So what discourse does the Other (singular or plural) appear in? In the form of a discourse addressed to people who are not Others. But where, then, do these Others come from? Are there Others, and if so, why? In order to clear up this mystery, we have to go back to the exhortation to accept them. Who is being invited to accept the Others? Not the Others, evidently. And who is making this call? We don't know their name, but we do know that they're not an Other. It is not the Other who asks for acceptance. But as well as not telling us their own name, they don't tell us who the 'Us' being addressed

---

5   *De l'existence à l'existant*, Paris: La Fontaine, 1947.

6   French for 'one another' is 'Les uns les autres' (literally 'The ones, the others') and Delphy is here playing on the implicit separation and opposition between the Ones and the Others – *translator's note*.

9

are. So behind this Other that we're always hearing about – without this Other ever speaking – is hidden another person, who speaks all the time, but who we never hear about: the 'One', who speaks to 'Us'. That is, the whole of society speaking to the whole of society. Normal society. Legitimate society. The society that's the same as the speaker who invites us to tolerate the Others. By definition, the Others are not ordinary people, because they are not 'Us'. So who is this 'One' who speaks? First of all, what we do know is that this One has the capacity to define the Other – because he does so. Then, this One adopts a position of tolerance or intolerance. But the One's capacity or power to define the Other precedes his adoption of either position. The Others, then, are the people whose lot it is to be defined as either acceptable or worthy of rejection, and, first of all, to be named as Others.

So *power* stands at the origin of the existence of Ones and Others – brute, simple, naked power, not power to be built or power to come but a power that already exists.

The mystery of the Other is thus resolved. The Other is whoever the One defines as the Other. The One is he who has the power to distinguish, to say what is what: who is a 'One', part of 'Us', and who is, instead, an 'Other', i.e., not part of 'Us'; he who has the power to catalogue, to class, in short, to name.

According to the psychological theory of 'consciences at war' (in which each conscience seeks the death of the other), this hatred is very much reciprocal. And even if this psychological theory were somewhat valid on its own terms, one of the main reasons why we cannot transpose it onto the societal plane – the principal reason being epistemological – is that in society the very thing that characterizes the relations between and even the definition of the One and the Other is the total lack of reciprocity. The Others – precisely because they are Others – cannot call the Ones 'Others'. But if we're dealing with 'difference' here, couldn't we say that the One is as different from the Other as the Other is from the One? Yes, of course. Both logically and on the school playground, the response to 'you're not like me' is 'no, it's you who aren't like me'. But that is just what Others cannot do: position themselves as the world's reference point, constructing Others of their own. This absence of reciprocity confirms the fact that the Other's status does not derive from what the Other is but from the Other's lack of power, in contrast with the power that the One does have.

This Other is never abused on account of the qualities or defects that the Other might display, either as an individual or as a group; rather, the Other is abused right from the outset, from the very moment of being defined as an 'Other'.

We must insist on this point, which is one of the central messages of my work, and which I have never ceased stating and restating in various ways. We often think of the oppression of one group by another in terms that imagine that these groups existed to start off with, before a power relation was established between them in which one group won out – often because the One is 'on home turf' while the Other is 'getting off the boat'. And the theory of the Other is largely used in this vein. But women never 'disembarked' in any human group. They were always there. So much for the theory of getting off the boat, then.

But we often say that men gave women an 'Othered' status. But men could not have done this if they did not exist already, surely? Why and how was this group 'men' created – along with its necessary antonym, the group 'women' – in a society in which the individuals who came to be called 'women' already concretely existed (albeit without the name)? Why and how did society divide into two opposed groups, one of which is held to be both contrary and complementary to the other, at the same time as one is superior and the other inferior?

Even if we accept that these groups pre-existed one of them being relegated to the status of an 'Other', then for women to let this happen, allowing the label 'Other' to be stuck on them, surely men must already have been stronger? So then we have to conclude that if men managed to dominate women, this was because . . . they already dominated them. So what's the point of the recourse to 'otherness'? Nothing. Or rather: 'otherness' is born of a hierarchical division, and is simultaneously the means of this division – evidently the inferior do not do the same as the superior do, unless having to follow their orders – and its justification: 'I'll drive the tractor while she chucks the bales onto the trailer with the pitchfork. Damn, it's a hard life being up in the driver's seat! What a drag!'

When for example Lévinas presents women or woman as the prototype of the Other, it is because he has already conceived of humanity – meaning 'I', meaning 'Us' – as necessarily but also *exclusively* composed of the group 'men'. To my right is humanity, and to my left, the instrument, the annex, the supplementary appendage of humanity, which is only there to 'help' it. When one group calls another 'the Other', it is already too late; it has already confiscated humanity, appropriating it as its own exclusive characteristic. But doesn't this suppose that the group 'men', for example, already existed prior to this appropriation? No – and not only does it not suppose this, but it supposes the very opposite: 'men' is the name given to the collection of individuals who have dispossessed all other human beings of their human quality. Just like the group 'whites' or 'heterosexuals'.

The hierarchy does not follow on from the division;[7] rather,

---

7   Christine Delphy, 'Penser le genre', talk given in December 1989 at the Sexe et Genre conference, CNRS, Paris. Published in M.C. Hurtig *et al.*, *Sexe et genre*, Paris: CNRS, 1991. Republished in *L'Ennemi principal*, Vol. II, 'Penser le genre', Paris: Syllepse, 2001.

it comes with it, or even a half-second before, as an intention. Groups are created simultaneously *both* in distinction *and* in a hierarchical order.

Discrimination: a way of life

The pieces presented in this book have not been brought together for the sake of studying the causes and mechanisms of the oppression of the three groups in question – women, homosexuals and non-whites. Rather, the only oppression on which I have worked in detail is the oppression of women. I do not claim to offer a theory of these three oppressions, nor – even less so – to compare them to each other.

I want to show just one aspect of these oppressions, an ideological and discursive element that is common to each of them and probably to all situations of domination. This ideological and discursive element is neither the only nor the central point of oppression. All oppressions have material causes and consequences. Moreover, discursive processes are not distinct from acts, but always accompany them and are themselves acts. For example, racism is not limited – as some 'specialists' would have it – to 'racial' or 'racialist', 'biological' or 'culturalist' theories underlying whites' 'prejudices' against black people, Arabs and Jews. Racism also – and even mainly – concerns what people confronted with *discrimination* suffer in each and every field; this discrimination, as with the hostility and violence that often accompany it, affects their material life, their conception of life, their confidence in other people, their optimism or pessimism regarding their future, and their self-esteem.

Only recently have we begun to take into account the victims as well as the real protagonists of racism, now considering it worth dwelling on what effects racism has on them. French researchers as well as French judges had been ignorant of the concept of discrimination, wanting to count only direct discrimination regarding the single individual and denying what the British and Americans had long understood: that discrimination is measured statistically. Looking at race, we pretended that such discrimination was now impossible since it is illegal to ask someone what race they are. But as concerned sex – which, on the contrary, it is compulsory to state – the statistics which would be so easy to obtain did not yet exist. It required Europe's intervention – in this matter like so many others – literally to force France to produce statistics for each sex, and they clearly demonstrated patriarchal discrimination. The continued refusal to give 'statistics according to ethnicity' is not motivated by the stated reasons but rather profound social and cultural factors. If even the concept of discrimination suited neither researchers nor judges, this was because it is not understood in our culture as something morally dubious, but as the 'normal' way of living one's life. We live in a universe where it is not only normal to prefer one individual to another, a family member to a stranger, a man to a woman, a 'true' Frenchman to an 'Arab' (a 'plastic Frenchman'), but where all this is part of each and every boss's prerogatives, following their instincts to make sure that everyone knows their place and the social order is respected, with Arabs doing 'Arabs' work' and women doing 'women's work'. But suddenly now they are told that what they are doing – with such a strong sense of moral righteousness and social virtue – is not only morally reprehensible but also perhaps legally dubious. A whole chunk of our values, of our representation of the world, such as it is and must be, crumbles.

Even to accept the notion that discrimination exists – that is to say, accepting that a woman or black person ought to be considered the equal of a man or a white person – represents a cultural shift for the white and male populations of France: it is quite simply 'the world turned upside down'. But this new norm is not only a 180-degree turn culturally speaking: it also raises the spectre of this male and white population losing the benefits it draws from discrimination. Indeed, rather than 'discrimination against . . .' – implying that some lose out, but not that anyone profits – it would be more accurate to speak of the advantages that some people gain and which are the stakes of this discrimination, by referring to 'preferential treatment' for men and for whites. This preferential treatment guarantees men and whites decision-making jobs, management jobs,[8] indeed, jobs of any kind[9] when they are in short supply. Moreover, to speak of preferential treatment better accounts for the manner in which different actors experience these processes of choice.

The making of the Other

Let's go back to the discursive and ideological processes I mentioned earlier: and by that I don't mean racist, sexist or homophobic opinions. The master group, the group of Ones, is not the same for all these three oppressions: for women it is men, for homosexuals it is heterosexuals, for 'non-whites' it is whites. However, in each case the master group has the same rhetoric: it reproaches its 'own' others (women for men, non-whites for whites, etc.) for not being part of the Ones, as if this were entirely their own doing. It reproaches them for being different, for not being 'the same', and exhorts them to be more 'similar' if they want to obtain their rights.

---

8   A woman in a small rural town: 'Oh yes! My son's doing very well, he's twenty years old and he's already ordering two Arabs around.' Here, Arab is synonymous with agricultural labourer. Indeed, having begun as a simple labourer at age twenty, the Arab is still in the same position forty-five years later.

9   The owner of a hotel-restaurant in another small rural town: 'I can't take on who I'd like to: for instance, I couldn't hire a Maghrebian so long as there are still local boys without a job' (the young Maghrebians are also born locally, but that doesn't make them 'local boys').

Yet the differences for which they are reproached are entirely constructed by the master groups; and in a number of ways. They are constructed ideologically, as one of their physical or behavioural characteristics is posed not as one of the countless traits that make individuals distinct from other individuals, but as a marker defining the boundary between superior and inferior. More precisely, one of the countless characteristics of humanity is posed as an axis with two opposite extremes: one good, one bad. Sometimes there are only two positions on this axis, for instance in the case of gender. The marker of this dimension – sex – is not clearly divided in two. When a baby is born a hermaphrodite, which happens much more often than we think and takes many more forms than we imagine, we 'rectify' its sex through surgery,[10] at the cost of a number of operations and much suffering for the children involved, such that its sex resembles a 'normal' sex, that is, one sex or the other.

In the case of skin colour, there are two possible solutions. We can either construct a clearly bipolar racial division as in the United States, where 'one drop of black blood (sic)' makes you a member of the inferior group; or else construct a graded hierarchy like in Brazil, where your degree of whiteness determines your social rank. Or rather, it apparently works by degrees; because there is still just one axis – colour – and just one colour, with just two poles: more white or more black, the former above and the latter below.[11] These markers of race or gender are more or less official: so your sex is written on your ID or your passport; not only is it legitimate to ask about it, but no interaction or transaction can take place without the

---

10 See *Nouvelles Questions féministes*, 27/1, 2008, 'À qui appartiennent nos corps, féminisme et luttes intersexes'.

11 Alexandra Poli, 'Faire face au racisme en France et au Brésil: de la condamnation morale à l'aide aux victimes', *Cultures & Conflits*, 59 – Dialogues franco-brésiliens sur la violence et la démocratie, Autumn 2005.

person's sex being identified.[12] In the United States racial clas-
sification is also compulsory – the superior race being called
'Caucasian' for the purposes of euphemism – but its mention
is less 'obligatory' than that of sex. As for France, in the
Caribbean race is dealt with in the same manner as Brazil – on
a scale – while in metropolitan France the situation is closer
to the American model – all or nothing; but the question must
be kept more informal than it is in the US, and it is forbidden
to address it openly. Declaring one's colour – unlike declaring
one's sex – is not only not allowed, but explicitly forbidden.
This allows the eradication of the very basis of this question:
in France there are no races, *so* there are no racial problems.
But race has no need for French sophistry; and while it does
not exist biologically or officially, it does exist as a social
marker labelling those who are not white, or black, or 'mixed
race'. I use the term 'race' in order to designate not a significant genetic – or, more broadly, natural – reality, but a social
construct that uses some of the morphological characteristics
of certain individuals in order to construct hierarchically
ordered groups, much as gender does for sex. The fact that
race is a social construct does not make it any less real – it is
even more real than any physical phenomenon ignored by
society. So I'm using the words 'racial, race, white, black,
Arabs, etc.' in a political sense. The British resolve this problem
by calling all non-whites – West Indians, Africans, Indians,
Pakistanis, Arabs – 'black', which does have the merit of simplicity and logic. In France we've created a special race just for
Arabs, as distinct from blacks, much like the distinction of
Latinos in the United States.

---

12   Trying to make a donation to Médecins du Monde, I filled out an
online form, duly providing my name as well as my postal and email
addresses, but that wasn't enough to be able to send the money: the pay-
ment was interrupted, and a screen appeared saying 'Sex is missing'.

As concerns homosexuals, it is even more difficult to identify them, because just as black Americans who have no more
than a single 'drop of black blood' can 'pass' (pass as whites,
at the cost of breaking with their whole past life, family,
friends and neighbourhood for the rest of their days),[13] gays
can easily 'pass' as heterosexuals, also at great cost to them.
(Detecting gays trying to 'pass' as straight is a popular pastime
among heterosexuals, just as much fun as a treasure hunt or
going hare-coursing.)

Next, the oppression to which the Others are subject *creates*
differences in reality: the dominated cannot behave, think or
act like the dominant, except at the cost of very quickly being
in the wrong or risking their lives. The dominated are always
on edge; never knowing on which foot to dance in their
everyday interactions; never knowing what to expect from the
next dominant person who crosses their path, and whether
they have to get ready to be smiled at or sneered at; never
knowing when or from whom insults, disdain and assault will
come next. Worse still, they never know whether they are being
discriminated against or not: was it because I am a woman,
an Arab, black or gay that I didn't get it – the apartment, the
promotion, the table in the restaurant – or was it because I'm
me? The Other's life is characterized by uncertainty over how
to interpret each interaction, with a permanent, exhausting
doubt about the meaning *of what is happening right now.*
That's why some of the sexist, racist and homophobic stereotypes about fearful and/or obsequious women, hypersensitive
(and obsequious) gays, easily provoked (and obsequious)
blacks and paranoid (and obsequious) Arabs are not without
some grain of truth.

Is this anything to be shocked about? No more than the fact
that men, heterosexuals and whites are disproportionately

13   Philip Roth, *La Tache*, Paris: Gallimard, 2002.

– and unduly – sure of themselves, arrogant and talkative: their socialisation and experience have made them like that, and their position allows it.

Othering [*altérisation*] thus alters the personalities of the dominated. But in France the 'great' specialists of racism have never addressed the psychic suffering among the oppressed, the effects of years of humiliations building up day after day. Even if some have begun studying discrimination, the dominant cannot even begin to imagine the suffering of its victims. After all, othering also alters the dominant – no one is the same as they would be if domination did not exist – but in an inverse sense; it creates dominant personalities. The characteristics of the dominant are not seen as specific characteristics, but as the way to be . . . normal. Of course, they are no more normal than the characteristics of the dominated. But the dominant demand that the dominated . . . be like them. And if you don't play along, well, then it's only normal that you don't have the right – among other things – to vote, drive, get a promotion, have a decent home, get a job suiting your qualifications, walk around without your papers, be out late at night, etc.

But how could the Others be like the Ones, when the Ones are only Ones because they oppress the Others?

This fact is constantly being denied and contradicted. The ways (of talking, of standing, of walking, of eating, etc.) of the dominant group are not presented for what they are – as ways that can only exist through domination – but as the norm, as the universal. And since the Ones' ability to have these ways is built on the oppression of the Others, it is meaningless to suggest that the Others could ever imitate them – not tomorrow, not in a thousand years. The Others will never manage to fit into what is presented as a universal norm that goes for everyone and which everyone can live up to. Something that results from the Ones' othering and alteration of these people is interpreted as these Others' own failing, and in any case their responsibility. Meanwhile, the Ones' privileges – won on the backs of the Others – instead appear as the proper recompense for their capacity to live up to the norm.

From insolence to communitarianism: when the Others name themselves

There is one further both discursive and ideological element common among all the situations where one group is arbitrarily set apart – socially marginalized on the symbolic terrain and discriminated against, exploited and physically and psychologically abused on the material terrain. This common element is the concern and hostility among the dominant groups when the Others become conscious of this situation, and publicly rebel.

In France there are thousands of different and diverse associations, hundreds of political groups ranging from twelve to 120,000 members, dozens of trade unions, professional orders, philanthropic associations, secret societies, churches and hundreds of religious denominations amounting to millions of believers – in short, an infinite mass of groups where individuals join together over the most varied affinities and for the most diverse goals. And still, there are still not enough intermediaries between state and citizen, and many politicians wish that the counter-powers to the state were stronger.

Few citizens would disagree with all this. However, when women, or gays, or 'people from an immigrant background' (non-whites) decide to meet in a public square to assert their demands for equality, their boldness provokes a scandal. The groups that bring together the oppressed – unlike the notorious organizations of the dominant, like Medef [French employers' association] – are accused of posing a threat to the Republic. We fear 'communitarianism'; not that anyone ever gives any definition of this, but we see it at work in the fact that blacks and Arabs 'choose to stick to their own kind', that is, with other unemployed people in the high-rise housing estates of Seine-Saint-Denis twenty miles from Paris rather than coming to mix in with 'Us' in the centre of the capital. These are people who never respond to invitations to dinner parties in Auteuil or Passy [very wealthy parts of Paris]. The same fear of homosexual 'communitarianism' reared its head when the number of gay bars in Le Marais became 'a concern'. Some people asked if 'straight people would feel at ease' in these gay bars. A good question: one that it's forbidden to turn the other way around.

A few years ago, one of those little 'miscellaneous' news items told us that a café in the south of France refused entry to North Africans. Journalists described this situation as if it were just how things are, not showing the slightest indignation or finding out if by chance this 'ban' might be illegal.

The Ones are those who have the right to close their door to whomever they like, to stay among their own kind, but who demand the right to go wherever they like and to feel at ease everywhere. The Others are those who are always too many in number, who are welcome nowhere, except perhaps among themselves, in a space often limited to their own home – and not even there, in women's case.

When the *Appel des Indigènes de la république* came out in January 2005,[14] I was surprised by the number of aggressive reactions, and also by their provenance, often coming from the Left, the far Left and anti-racist movements. I saw the same hostility – or worse, if that is possible – that the women's liberation movement had faced when it was created. And the same critiques came up all over again; we often read that they

---

14 www.indigenes-republique.org/spip.php?article85.

(the *indigènes*)[15] were not entirely wrong in what they were criticizing, but, heaven above – how badly they put it! It was also much too abstract, or, on the contrary, much too emotional. Unsurprising, that – you'd have thought that those who wrote it would have felt personally concerned. This flagrant lack of objectivity was blindingly obvious to all the whites who nonetheless felt so much sympathy for this cause. 'Why didn't you tell me about this in advance?', one of them wrote, 'I could have written the Appeal for you!' Others helpfully pointed out what the authors' (normal enough) lack of culture had clearly prevented them from understanding: that the code of '*indigénat*' no longer existed in the France of 2005. Oh, please . . . using the word *indigènes*? It's us who give them their names, we have always given them names, plenty of names (and today their name is 'immigrants and their descendants', or even 'the products of diversity' – let's not have any fear of ridicule). But *indigènes*? – seriously, now!

I could hardly believe that thirty-five years after the birth of second-wave feminism we were hearing the same arguments against the unity of the oppressed that I had criticized in 'Nos amis et nous' in 1977.[16] The argument most on display was the same as what had been said about women's liberation in 1970: 'There is no racial question, there is just one question, the "social question". All possible and imaginable oppressions are reducible to capitalist exploitation and dissolve into it.'

We might have hoped that after thirty-five years the far Left might have learnt a few things – but no. The implicit argument

---

15   '*Les indigènes*' is the French word for natives. There was a special law for them which took justice out of the hands of judges and put it in the hands of administrators. This *code de l'indigénat* was applied in all French colonies until 1945.

16   'Nos amis et nous, des fondements réels de quelques discours pseudo-féministes', *Questions Féministes*, November 1977, republished in *L'Ennemi principal*, Vol. I.

hidden behind this museum piece of a refrain is that the oppressed do not have the intellectual means to analyse their situation correctly. They can provide raw, even moving testimony, for sure; but when it comes to analysing this experience, they have to step aside and give way to those who know what they're doing. The only defence of the *Appel des Indigènes* was that in spite of its failings it could at least be 'considered a kind of cry for help'. A cry: a human noise, albeit an inarticulate one. Accepting that it was an appeal for help: the least critical voices could go that far, 'saving' it from the general reprobation. Its theoretical framework and the rigour of its argumentation were erased, denied and went unseen. But why, if not because it came from the oppressed?

Thirty years after the rebirth of the feminist movement worldwide, at a time when there was an impressive volume of feminist books and articles analysing women's oppression in every language, or almost all of them, Pierre Bourdieu claimed in his *Masculine Domination* that women were so alienated – precisely because they are dominated – that they could not even think their situation. He, however, could do so. Why? Because he was, or saw himself, as impartial – in short, a neutral observer, not playing any part in the oppression of women, though he did call it 'masculine domination'. Maybe he ought to have understood that since he is part of the group 'men', he couldn't be impartial? Indeed, that no one could be impartial or objective, because everyone is a woman or a man? Of course, he knew that he was a man; but not only did he not think that this would stop him being objective, but that men, not being 'alienated' by the oppression of women, were better placed to analyse it. This is a typical attitude of the dominant, seeing others – and above all, Others – as partisan, wanting to be their own 'judge, jury and executioner'. Conversely, they conceive their own dominant group – who are of course also 'party' to the case – as impartial 'judges'.

Perhaps it's that they see themselves as somehow external to this hierarchy, even though they also recognize that they occupy its top rung?[17]

Not exactly. From birth the Ones have been raised in the belief – and it's an integral part of them, because it flows from their dominant position – that nothing human is foreign to them and nothing *should* be. They have the deeply rooted conviction that they embody the *whole* human condition; moreover, that they are the *only* people who can embody it; and furthermore, that they can do it alone – to the point that many fine authors over the centuries, including Auguste Comte, have asked themselves why the hell humanity was encumbered with women when other means for its reproduction – that is, the reproduction of men only – could surely have been thought up. This belief is perfectly captured in Lévinas's formula, and it also dictates Bourdieu's pig-headed attitudes.

The dominant are unable to shake off these attitudes; not only on account of being brought up in the aforementioned belief, but also because such an approach directly serves their own interests. So while we can all recognize that the oppression of women exists, we really ought not say that it benefits all men, because there are nice ones as well as bad. And yes, the oppression of blacks and Arabs does exist, but we ought not say that it benefits all whites; after all, are not anti-racists – as identified by their belonging to parties or organizations declaring themselves anti-racist – all automatically excluded from benefiting? And once all these are discounted, there's not many people left, except National Front voters. And as for identifying the agents or beneficiaries of the oppression of

---

17 There's a notable difference between Bourdieu's treatment of gays' and of women's writings. When he encountered the gay movement he credited it for its relevance and even its inventiveness. Of course, in *that* movement there are men . . .

homosexuals . . . and yet the insult 'cocksucker' is one of the first words that male children learn.

I was also surprised by the anger that flared up among whites when the word 'white' was used. But not for long. I remember very well the reactions in the feminist movement when gay women said that they wanted to have non-mixed meetings, among themselves. Married women had their meeting one night a week and were active alongside other women the rest of the time; no one raised an eyebrow when they said they were going to do this. We simply wanted to do likewise. The outcry that our announcement provoked led to interminable discussions – in twos, in threes, collectively. How would we be able to tell who was a gay woman [*homosexuelle*] (the term used at the time, before the rehabilitation of the word 'lesbian'), we were asked with derision; would they have to show their membership cards?

What I clearly saw at the end of a month of discussions was that the heterosexual women did not want to be catalogued, they didn't want to be given a name, and they especially didn't want anyone other than themselves attributing a name to them. We can identify two different aspects of this complaint. The first is a rejection of being confined within an identity. Indeed, the dominant, who think that they are everywhere at home, think that they can choose whatever social position and change it however they please: all possibilities are always open to them. No place and no social position is shut off to them *a priori*. That they don't always make use of them in practice is neither here nor there. What is at issue here is their representation of themselves as essentially and by definition *free*, as against those people who – unfortunately for them – are limited by, confined by, and boil down to their 'specificities'; and who are obliged, as in the case of gay women, to put up with the labels stuck on their backs without anyone asking their opinion. The other aspect of this complaint is that when the

Other, the inferior, the black, the woman, the poof and the dyke name the dominant, they are usurping their privilege. After all, it's their privilege to name individuals, to sort them into categories independently of what those concerned say or want; to *class* them. For to class people is to establish a hierarchy. And no name is neutral – 'gay woman' is not a description; it is the name of an inferior social category. That's what we do to the Other. That is how We (the Ones) show that the Other is an Other.

When the Other turns this process around – implying reciprocity, when this process is by definition not reciprocal – s/he shakes up the rules of the game, symbolically at least challenging the whole organization of society. After all, the dominated are dominated, so to say, on account of their *specific* characteristics; but naming the dominant means specifying them, too. And it specifies them in a way that erases their superiority (on the symbolic plane, still): the names given are formally equal, at least from the point of view of anyone's pretentions to universality; 'white' is just as particular as 'black' or 'gay'. To replace the opposition between 'general' and 'specific' with the opposition between two specificities is unbearable, it means –

To attack the taboo of all taboos, the sacred: the Ones' stranglehold on the universal[18]

– For the dominant, this is unbearable. We had a further example of this with the furore that Houria Bouteldja provoked when she said during a TV show[19] that she called people

---

18 Perhaps the gay and lesbian movements' greatest victory is a symbolic one: the fact that 'heterosexuals' now call themselves the name that homosexuals gave them. That does not, however, mean that they see this condition as a particularism of similar peculiarity to being homosexual.

19 'These upholders of "*souchien*" order" nonetheless intuitively

of French stock [*Français de souche*] 'Souchiens' [a pun on 'sous-chiens', lower than dogs].

Many think that this furore was all a misunderstanding, on account of some people having imagined that she meant to say 'sous-chiens'. But in fact, when the media and the minister of identity leapt into the fray, it was not because they didn't understand, but, on the contrary, because they understood perfectly. In rationalizing the expression 'Français de souche', giving it a typical French grammatical form for an adjective indicating place or nationality – a term ending in 'ien' (*Italien, Canadien, Australien,* etc.) – Bouteldja demonstrated its absurdity. She brought to the fore what many people already felt, confusedly – 'to what "stock" does this refer?', the Hernandezes, Gianninis and Finkielkrauts asked themselves. Even so, most people content themselves with saying that it doesn't actually concern people's origin; that the mirror-image term 'immigrants and their descendants' doesn't apply to them, even if they, too, are descended from immigrants; that this latter is a euphemism for blacks and Arabs; and contenting themselves with the fact – which they can be certain of, for nothing is better known than racial appellations, even disguised ones – that in reality 'people of French stock' means whites, and that they are part of this group (phew!). Moreover, the term 'white' does not describe the real skin colour of the people to whom it refers, as it suggests. Rather, it is a linguistic convention denoting who is dominant in a dichotomous, hierarchical system in which the dominant appeal to physical notions (including notions of colour) in order to identify and name the Others; and this term is itself shocking for those concerned, insofar as it was 'invented' by their inferiors.

We can ask ourselves if all the categorizations that exist in

---

understood that in redefining them, this neologism jeopardized their privilege': http://bougnoulosophe.blogspot.com.

a society are necessarily and inevitably hierarchical. Many researchers in the social sciences think that we cannot do without categories and that categorizing responds to the need to describe individuals more quickly and easily by attaching them to groups whose characteristics we know already. As I said in the preface to the second volume of *L'Ennemi principal*, the identification of groups – differentiating whole cohorts of individuals or items – is not necessarily hierarchical; for example, the description 'vegetables' does not order cauliflowers, carrots, leeks and aubergines in a hierarchical manner. However, it's different when this categorization is dichotomous as well as comprehensive; when all vegetables or all human beings are classed in a categorization that only recognizes two terms, and from which no vegetable or human can escape. If not belonging to one category is the same thing as belonging to the other, then the goal of this characterization is, indeed, to set them in a hierarchical order. One of the categories is necessarily superior, and the other necessarily inferior to it. Perhaps these categorizations could survive and yet cease to be hierarchical, no longer privileging the Ones and stigmatizing the Others? My answer to that is a 'no', since I cannot find any example of it in social reality (I'll just have to stick to my vegetables, it seems). In fact, every possible and imaginable trait is preceded by a plus sign or a minus sign (however lightly it is pencilled in).

A guide for the reader
A last word on this collection. I made these precise texts into a single volume because for me, given my political and intellectual journey, it made perfect sense for them to go together. To shed some light on them, for my readers' benefit, I ought to say a little something about this journey. I first encountered the struggle against racism in the United States, where I was a student at the high point of the black Civil

Rights struggle. Moreover, I abandoned university in the third year of my stay, in order to work for the oldest black Civil Rights organization (together with the NAACP) active across the US, the National Urban League. In the same period I read everything by Freud, and his pseudo-scientific judgements on the normality of heterosexuality had the paradoxical effect of making me understand that negative views of homosexuality were just as arbitrary and indefensible as anti-Semitism – and I said this to a Jewish friend, who didn't dare to contradict me, but was left open-mouthed. In this Civil Rights organization I was on the sharp end of what we would now call sexual harassment by my boss, and I thought: from now on I'll only work for my people – that is, women – whose oppression seemed to me to be of the same order as racism, in the light of my analyses of the situation of the black population in the US.

I wanted a women's liberation movement, and thanks to May '68 I met other women and we founded one of the first feminist groups, FMA (Féminin masculin avenir, which became Feminisme marxisme action in 1969). And, much later, I rediscovered racism, so to speak. But it didn't come 'from the inside', as we sometimes say in politics; rather, the first Gulf War gave me a terrible shock. I couldn't believe that the entire West would go to war against a country while there was still so much room for negotiation; I couldn't believe that France, as represented by Mitterrand, declared this war inevitable – on account of the logic of war (sic). And not until the last moment, on the night that CNN correspondents hidden under a table broadcast the blaze of the first bombs dropped on Baghdad, did I believe that this nightmare would become reality. Many of us, hundreds of thousands of people in France and Germany, protested against this war. And then once Iraq was defeated and destroyed we heard nothing more about it, or almost nothing, through twelve years of sanctions. It was clear enough to me that no country populated by whites would have been treated like this (though Serbia did experience comparable treatment for a few weeks).[20] I was also angered by the light-mindedness with which people on the Left and feminists gargled with terms like 'just war'. To be able to say this, they must have been supremely indifferent to the fate of the Iraqi people during the war and the sanctions, and to the fact that civilians were dying because of the deliberate destruction of water management infrastructure and the embargo administrators' holding back of indispensable medical supplies. The Iraqis paid a heavy price for not being white; and also for being Arabs. During these years I noticed the right-wing drift of the media's appointed intellectuals, and the nagging refrain of the injunction they made week after week, month after month, year after year, for 'second-generation immigrants' to stop being delinquents and 'to integrate'. This, at the same time as the religion in which many of these latter believe was tirelessly decried in the media, week after week, month after month, as incompatible with democracy, with the Republic, in short, with civilization.[21]

I had not seen France as racist: rather, I thought the US had something of a monopoly on racism. But I was stupefied to hear of people being addressed as 'second-generation immigrants', as if the quality of being an immigrant could be inherited. I could not ignore that something was happening here without precedent in previous waves of immigration, better resembling the situation of the black descendants of slaves.

These exhortations to integration were rather curious: as

---

20 Interesting to note in this regard is that while in France Serbs are seen as whites, in Switzerland they are treated like Arabs are in France.

21 Thomas Deltombe, *L'Islam imaginaire: la construction médiatique de l'islamophobie en France (1975-2005)*, Paris: La Découverte, 2005.

of 1990 the majority of 'Arabs' in France were born in France, and were French. Much of the black population was from the French Caribbean or Réunion, their families having been French citizens across many generations. We could no longer explain this situation in terms of the syndrome of the most recently arriving immigrant group, nor in terms of xenophobia. In 2001 I wrote that racial castes were forming in France, as in the United States.[22]

That same year I had a further shock when Bush announced a 'war without end' against terrorism in revenge for the Twin Towers attack, starting with a war against Afghanistan. And I was also angered when the question of women wearing the burqa came up, without any good reason. I understood that the feminist movement had been manipulated. Together with some friends – both male and female – I formed a group to protest against this war, and for several months I worked on uploading news from foreign media to the site cicg.free.fr [CICG; 'International Coalition Against War'], in order to counter the disinformation to which we in France had fallen victim. In the first decade of the 2000s, American imperialism turned on the Middle East (though that did not mean leaving Latin America alone); and an increasingly negative image of Arabs and Muslims was propagated, with themes that matched up with Israeli propaganda. In France, this reactivated the racism that had justified the colonization of North Africa and then the economic exploitation of North Africans and their children.

After its victory over Afghanistan the US secretly smuggled 'suspects' to its base at Guantánamo Bay in Cuba. Guantánamo is a model example of how the powerful create categories. The United States kidnapped people wherever it pleased, all over the world, imprisoning them for life without trial and even

---

22   Preface to *L'Ennemi principal*, Vol. II.

without bringing charges. Then the Americans created a meaningless *ad hoc* category, 'enemy combatants' . . . though given that this term does not appear in the Geneva Convention, what it does designate is the people that the US kidnaps in defiance of this convention. That's all there is to it. I was angered by the deference with which the French media covered this matter (and still does today),[23] never mentioning its illegality. I also understood that this indifference resulted from racism as well as the media's feeble kowtowing to American policy; even though the French diplomatic corps was opposed to the war, the journalists were its fervent partisans. Conversely, the French government did nothing to help the French nationals imprisoned at Guantánamo – as was its duty – and when three of these men were released after three years, the French authorities immediately re-imprisoned them, unlike the British government, which had demanded the return of the detainees of British nationality and welcomed them back to British soil with apologies. But before this last infamy, I, together with the CICG, had made contact with the lawyers of the three French nationals, organizing a meeting on this matter in April 2002. This meeting had little success, with even people 'on the Left' judging this cause rather 'difficult'. I also found the way in which the kidnapped men were excluded from the category 'humanity' in just a few hours to be a model example of othering. They were subjected to physical brutalization and judicial (or rather, extra-judicial) treatment that exempted them from any of the international human rights conventions, starting with the Geneva Convention, without other countries raising any shadow of a protest.

---

23 Speaking of the defendant at the first Guantánamo trial, *Le Monde* commented on 30 July 2008 that 'Even if he is acquitted, he will not be released, because he has been classed an "enemy combatant". The Pentagon is still detaining 265 prisoners, and according to the military officials it will only be possible to press charges against 80 of them.'

In 2002, the American preparations for the war in Iraq forced Bush to come out of the woodwork and clearly designate the Muslim world as the enemy of the West: the Axis of Evil. These were all things that cut through French whites' consciousness like a knife through butter; after all, spitting on Arabs is a centuries-long tradition of theirs. A fresh war against Iraq was declared in 2003, and despite the UN's reservations, the country – or what was left of it – was destroyed for a second time. Western racism against Arabs and Muslims took the reins from traditional French racism. Besides, can it be any coincidence that it was in spring 2003, when the US's anger against France for having 'stabbed it in the back' – refusing to participate in the second war on Iraq – was at its height, that we had the third hubbub over the Islamic scarf? As we know, this was a slick operation that caught the whole nation's attentions at a moment when prime minister Raffarin was dismantling Social Security. The two or three hundred teenage women whose headscarves worn at school so tarnished French secularism were removed from classrooms. But was the important thing here some sort of threat to a secularism that had never until then prevented the expression of religious convictions – a secularism which, moreover, was not respected, and still isn't, in three mainland *départements* (in Alsace-Moselle) without anyone making any fuss about it – or was it that France should show that it was playing its role in the war on Muslims? Was the 'veil' (as the headscarf was renamed) affair not, in Chirac's head, a miniature Iraq war, waged on French territory against unarmed female high-school students? No doubt, because the American retaliation had been fierce, and it was worth falling into line; but in vain, because France's goodwill was misunderstood in the United States, where trampling on religious freedom – even Muslims' freedom – is looked upon unkindly.

During the second 'veil' affair in 1995, *Nouvelles Questions féministes* had expressed its opposition to the pupils' exclusion, and in 2003 this journal again took a position against the anti-headscarf law. There was even less question of reconsidering its position considering that anti-Arab and anti-Muslim propaganda had multiplied tenfold in the intervening eight years, and given that the law was passed on 15 March 2004 not because of the 'secular' or 'feminist' arguments springing up everywhere, but rather because of the floodgates of racism being opened wide in this period.

I took a public stance against this law because it is unjust; but also because France's strategy, consisting of repressing something that it accurately enough perceived as a way of challenging racism, seemed to me dated, inappropriate and counterproductive. Certainly there is not much risk in punishing, humiliating and arbitrarily treating a colonized population denied the most basic human rights. But what will the long-term results be when this formula is applied to French and European citizens, who know their rights and feel equal to all other citizens, and revolt precisely because *de jure* equality does not lead to *de facto* equality? When a whole group constituted by oppression, and thus by an oppressor, feels and knows itself to be under attack by this repression against the 'veiled girls'? When the master group, whites, responds to the protest against injustice with even more injustice?

I did not only react as a human. I also reacted as a white, seeing the racial group to which I belong (like it or not) giving grist to the mill of non-whites' legitimate grievances and thereby increasing their rancour. What are we doing? Have we gone mad? Do we want to create the conditions for a civil war? I asked myself these questions, and put them to my feminist comrades. Indeed, it was these events that attracted me to Une École pour toutes et tous [One School for All] and Féministes pour l'égalité [Feminists for Equality]. And we didn't have to

34

wait long for the beginnings of a response. Less than a year after this headscarf law, in 2005 the Indigènes de la Republique was set up – its radicalism and creativity reminding me of the first years of the feminist movement, followed by the CRAN [Representative Council of Black Associations] and many other grassroots initiatives that would soon change the French political landscape. In the autumn of that same year, the interior minister's lies over what caused the death of two '*banlieue*[24] kids' and then his verbal provocations associating these two victims with delinquency led to rioting that lasted three weeks.

I have above all taken positions as a feminist, because the 'women's cause' has been instrumentalized in a shameful way, and continues to be so, by the imperial war ('the war on terror') that is currently under way; curiously, many feminists seem not to have noticed. Or perhaps they do approve of this war, putting being white above being women?

Today these struggles do not all converge, and perhaps it is illusory to think that they will one day do so. However, we will not win our oppressors' indulgence by giving them our support, following them along other paths of oppression and othering. Would we even want to? We don't need their indulgence – we want justice.

---

24 Suburbs, often stereotyped in terms of ghettoization. Roughly similar to the US English term 'projects' or UK English 'council estates', though by definition they are in peripheral areas rather than in the inner cities – *translator's note*.

35

CHAPTER 2

For Equality: Affirmative Action Over Parity

Political parity is generally presented as the demand for perfect equality, with an equal number of men and women in elected assemblies and in the national parliament: recreating in the assembly halls the same proportions that exist among the general population.

In my view the demand for parity suffers from problems in the objective it sets, its argumentation and its tactics. Its failings deny it the support of a good part of the only forces that would be able to make something of it: feminist movements. But if its goal were reformulated in a broader sense, as the expansion of women's participation in decision-making across the whole of society and thus *also* in political assemblies – whether or not they are elected – then the reasoning behind it could also be different, with arguments anchored in universalism. Its tactic, instead of requiring an important legislative change, could, instead, not be dependent on this. Rather, it could be inscribed within the already-existing framework – in theory at least – of affirmative action. Finally, in order to win the support of the majority of feminists it could be simultaneously both more and less ambitious: women's access to positions of responsibility in political assemblies would no longer have to be presented as the panacea that it never could be. Conversely, locating this access within an affirmative action policy extending across all sectors of society and all fields of activity would silence the critiques asking what substantial programme would accompany the guarantee of women being elected to regional and national assemblies.

The demand for parity in access to political roles is not separate from the wider demand for access to all important functions and decision-making positions; and, moreover, access to all functions and all positions, high or low . . . though we need not demand these latter. The demand that a law be passed establishing a quota – a ½ quota is still a quota – is just as justified as any affirmative action policy; and quotas are one of the crucial tools of such a policy.

Is this affirmative action policy necessarily grounded in unacceptable assumptions, as some people say? Is it futile? Is it ultimately impossible – doomed to failure? That is some feminists' view, and they raise three orders of criticism against this demand:

1)   That this justification is essentialist, and that
1b) this essentialism, which feminism criticizes when it sees it in the dominant mode of thinking – meaning, the division of humanity into two distinct sub-species – can be found in the constitution and, at least, in the law;
2)   Democracy is itself masculine by essence and thus irretrievable;
3)   The election of women would not guarantee any progress for women.

I will seek firstly to find out whether these critiques are unanswerable – whether it is impossible to salvage the substantial proposition that the demand for parity expresses. I will then try to explain how affirmative action can be inscribed within the search for a true universalism.

On the one hand, the universalist stance that some use as a stick to beat dominated groups, in the name of resisting communitarianism, is in fact a defence of the monopolization of universalism by one very specific group of the population – white men.

On the other hand, this resistance to excluded groups' protests – which in France takes the form of invoking grand principles, thus turning the doctrine of human rights against . . . human rights – is not without its effects on the form taken by the demands of those excluded from citizenship, including women. The dominant groups' incapacity to understand that the time has come for them to abandon their monopoly control of the universal, as well as their refusal to give in to the excluded's demand for a real universal – that is, an inclusive one – are responsible for the situation of conflict that could lead to the dismantling of the republican form. After all, the dominated knocked at the door of a house that they were told was common property, but did not meet with success. They were told that this house is not in fact theirs, and that they can only enter if they are invited in: so they may well prefer to abandon it to those who claim to be its only legitimate owners, and begin to look elsewhere. That is to say, they will start to take a closer look at the red rag that the dominant wave in front of every protest: that is, 'communitarianism', or separatism – in any case, a parallel path that will be of no good for either them or the rest of the nation.

Affirmative action is preferable to parity
1) *Parity's goals are compatible with a non-essentialist analysis*
The partisans of parity sometimes deploy an essentialist kind of reasoning. It often invokes the need for women to be 'represented', in function of their essential natural difference from men. Sex difference, in this view, is incomparable to any other social difference. While the separate or specific representation of other social groups is impermissible, it does make sense in the case of men and women, according to this argument.

The demand for parity thus leads us to the question 'What

makes men and women?' just as people used to say, 'What makes a foot soldier's feet?' The answer back then was 'a foot soldier's feet are the object of constant attention'. Similarly, the system formed by the division between men and women, the gender system, is the object of the constant attentions of society as such, and of each of its members.

What is this gender system? It is the cognitive system that separates humanity into two totally distinct, impermeable groups, each excluding the other and standing in rigorous hierarchy.[1] In this sense, the gender system is distinct from the 'classic' class system. However, it is based on a classed organization of society: a hierarchy of sex classes, or gender classes. This social organization, in which women are oppressed and exploited as a group by the other half of humanity, is called patriarchy. The gender system is thus the cognitive aspect of patriarchy – a political-economic form of organization – while sexism is their common ideology.

What is gender? As a concept, it more or less corresponds to 'social sex'. Research has shown that the majority of the differences between the sexes – the differences in their social status, wealth and power, but also the differences between men's and women's so-called 'psychology', attitudes and aptitudes – are not caused by anatomical sex or the different roles in procreation that result. Indeed, the sole consequence of anatomical sex is that men and women play different roles in procreation. So all the rest – which is commonly called sex difference and typically explained in terms of anatomy – is a social construct. According to some, the reason behind this social construct can be found in men's and women's different roles in procreation. For others, including myself, the anatomical difference is just a marker, a distinctive trait that makes it

---

1   Christine Delphy, 'Penser le genre: quels problèmes?', in M.C. Hurtig *et al.* (eds.), *Sexe et genre*, Paris: Éditions du CNRS, 1991.

easier to identify the people to exploit. This is today considered a bold claim, but I am sure that one day it will be taken as a given.

Whether we consider this gender system to originate in anatomical difference and its consequences for procreation or, like me, in hierarchy itself, all feminists are united in condemning this hierarchy. In short, whether we consider gender to be inherently linked to sex or not, we agree that it is a social construct produced by an unjust political and economic order. And the demand for parity can be based on an analysis built on gender: it does not necessarily have to be essentialist. However, we ought to distinguish between parity posed in terms of access to elected office or political assemblies more generally (whether or not they are elected) and parity as a form of representation.

An analysis based on gender does justify increasing women's access to positions from which we have been excluded: it is simply the implementation of a non-discriminatory policy, and a non-discriminatory policy can and should proceed by way of affirmative action, sometimes called positive discrimination. It doesn't much matter what we call it: in any case, it is an effort to correct a past discrimination whose effects we feel still today, and correct present discriminations – be they *de jure* or *de facto* – that prevent some people from having equal opportunities on account of the group to which they belong. Such is the philosophy of affirmative action, wherever it is practised. This is the UN's philosophy, indeed: it holds that affirmative action cannot be seen as a form of discrimination. In this view it is at odds with the French Constitutional Council as well as the last decree from the European Court; but international conventions count for more than national laws or European decisions, and so we can hope that France and Europe will soon be putting their house in order.

Indeed, the UN doctrine – already adopted by the US and

Canada – is happy to note that there are oppressed groups in society and formally recognize this, arguing that not to recognize it amounts to defending the oppressive situation. This doctrine, developed by its Human Rights Committee, represents the most advanced reflection on what the French still call – not by chance – 'the rights of man', thus excluding women, when in all other languages they are called human rights.

As such, while the fact that some arguments for parity are essentialist may invalidate these particular arguments, it does not detract from the demand itself. After all, it can just as legitimately be based on another kind of reasoning.

1b) *Transforming the demand for parity into a demand for quotas* would remove the obstacle of needing to pass legislation – because whatever the French courts might think, affirmative action quotas are perfectly legitimate according to international treaties. Moreover, it would remove the hypothetical problem of writing gender into law, which would be paradoxical from the perspective of those feminists – including myself – whose struggle's ultimate goal is not to consolidate gender but rather to abolish it.

2) *According to some feminist analysts, modern democracy is founded on the solidarity among men*, which is itself based on the exclusion of women. Insofar as democracy as an institution is coextensive with the exclusion of women, then by definition it would be impossible to bring women into it. Even so, the manner in which an institution is established can be either structural or accidental. The notion of democracy does not imply the exclusion of anyone or any group. It is the case that in the American and French republics emerging from the Enlightenment, solidarity among citizens was built on solidarity among men, founded on their common status as patriarchs; firstly as owners of women, children and

commodities – in French democracy, the franchise, reserved to men, was also for a long time based on property qualifications. However, the abandonment of the property qualification did not spell the end of the Republic. Similarly, since marriage no longer means – in law at least – that the wife is the property of the husband, there is no need today for the solidarity among citizens to be founded on a common status of wife-ownership.

We could argue that democracy rests on exclusion. But it is paradoxical for the opponents of parity to use this argument, since the logical conclusion of this analysis would have to be the repudiation of democracy as a charade and an illusion, and the demand that those excluded from this masquerade be accorded parallel authorities in this same territory. But we could also argue that real democracy has never conformed with the principles that it invokes: as soon as these principles were formulated, the people who controlled the real body politic hurried to make exceptions to them, excluding first women and then propertyless males from the *res publica*. The problem, here, resides in the incarnations of democracy and the fact that one or several specific classes monopolize them – not the principles themselves. And these principles have the particular advantage of providing a basis with which to criticize their real-world application. Ultimately, the challenge to how the Republic functions is being made in the name of its own principles.

3) *Parity for what purpose?*, or, 'Will women defend women's interests'? I am sensitive to this question, and sometimes pessimistic about the answer. But we ought to consider that the alternative is changing nothing, leaving some assemblies – the French parliament, particularly so – with a male composition bordering on 95 per cent. Women are not necessarily feminist, but the probability that they are is greater than the probability

that men will be. So nothing could be worse than the present situation – and there's everything to gain and nothing to lose in changing it.

Moreover, we ought to revisit the distinction between access and representation, a distinction that is not made often enough and is rather a nuisance for the partisans of parity. After all, sometimes they say that 'It would be good for women, because women wouldn't do the same things as men' – and they are then accused of essentialism, in thinking that women are good by nature, or else of the sin of naivety, in believing that women would necessarily have other women's interests at heart. Or they say, 'We can't promise you anything,' and they are accused of cynicism, meeting with the answer, 'Then why should we vote for you?'

I believe that we need to draw a sharp division between *access* and *representation*.

Women should be treated equally to men – who do not have to be feminists – and be able to reach positions without having any extra requirements placed on them. Indeed, this is the classic form of discrimination, having to 'deserve' what others are entitled to.

Of course, it would be better for all women's status if feminists were elected. But that depends on women voters as much as on women candidates, if not more so. Women in France do not make their voice heard with their vote, unlike in other countries where there is a women's vote: that is, a significant difference between women's and men's votes (a gender gap) showing that women are conscious of their specific interests. That is what we're missing in France.

False universalism – or, the masculine neuter
1) *France's identitarian retreat; or, the defence of privilege*
    Affirmative action has provoked strong resistance in France. This resistance cannot be explained except in terms of the

defence of the dominant groups' privileges. This defence takes the form of a demonization of the United States and an idealization of France. The demonization of America is achieved through an active disinformation campaign regarding what is taking place there, disinformation that uses caricatures – or even pure and simple inventions – that the whole of French society accepts as the reality. In 1996, when sexual harassment became a crime in France as well as the US, we could read in a paper of *Le Monde*'s standing that in America, 'looking at someone the wrong way can get you taken to court'. It was in 1994 that I first heard a participant in a TV debate saying that 'today in America men are afraid of getting into an elevator alone with a woman'. He spouted this bullshit as if it were a proven scientific fact. After that, I heard it being repeated at least twenty times – this phrase became a commonplace, an evangelical truth. People who have never set foot in the US or Canada, who have never read a single word of a single article written in English, tell you, 'I know what America's like – it's like this'. Their information comes exclusively from the French press. These papers have few correspondents – and it's always the same ones – who write what the French apparently want to read: that America is a country of intense police repression at the same time as drugs are openly on sale in the streets, a country of lasciviousness and puritanism at the same time as child rapists (until recently the only telefilms dealing with incest were American ones) and unjustifiable sexual harassment cases pervade society. Media-appointed intellectuals come on the TV to denounce America's puritanism and communitarianism ... In short, the US is everything and its opposite, but always hellish.

These myths and exaggerations could just be the amusing trivia of French provincialism, if not for the fact that their authors are inspired by the most reactionary wing of the American Right, and if these authors didn't present themselves as progressives – profiting from a reputation that they haven't done anything to earn for some decades. On the contrary, they are engaged in a dubious struggle against the most progressive aspects of US society.

They accompany this denunciation of all things American with their defence of an ideal model, which just so happens to be the French model, of which we in France are the sole proprietors. On this point there is an interesting convergence of Left and Right: they are strikingly in agreement, whatever the other disputes they may have, as to the urgent need always and everywhere to eulogize France, the homeland of human rights, democracy, universalism and Camembert. Which is evidently false from a historical and factual point of view (well, OK, cheese excepted). We do not have a monopoly on unselfish ideas, nor on any of these other things. But this French craze for self-congratulation is getting noisier. Take the example of 'cultural exception' – an expression coined during the GATT negotiations, meaning that all cultural production was exempt from the agreement. After a rather revealing collective mistranslation of this term, it became 'French cultural exception' and then 'French exceptionalism'. The French feeling of superiority has never been more pronounced,[2] at a time when France is increasingly cut off from the rest of the world. After all, when the foreign media talk about French exceptionalism, they don't mean it as a compliment. But the French are unaware of this, or else do not care. When they hear the criticisms levelled against France, they do not tone down their self-satisfaction; quite the opposite. It merely feeds a persecution complex, reinforcing the French sense of self-righteousness. The monopolization of values that belong to all humanity; the heroic portrayal of the nation resisting assault from abroad; a

---

2 Christine Delphy, 'L'affaire Hill-Thomas et l'identité nationale française', *Nouvelles Questions féministes*, 14/4, 1993.

self-righteous and combative sense of isolation; jeremiads on the misunderstandings to which it falls victim; who cannot recognize, in all this, the mental and ideological processes of nationalism?

So the pseudo-progressive media intellectuals are the agents or echoes of a sort of 'Left' nationalism. It appeals not to Joan of Arc but to the French Revolution, which as it happens is not attacked 'from abroad', though nor is it considered the perfect realization of human progress.

This form of Left nationalism – which is less and less different from the nationalism of the Right – is accompanied by an attack on all dissenting groups: ethnic minorities, feminists and gays, accused of wanting to destroy national unity and republican universalism. We can look at this phenomenon in two different ways: either this attack is the real political goal of this nationalist approach; or else the nationalism and the attack against 'minorities' are an indissoluble whole, the contraction of national identity to an ever-narrower norm. After all, the fight against domestic dissidents, the sense of a culture endangered and identitarian retreat are all characteristic of nationalism.

Whatever the case, some further questions remain: what universalism is it exactly that these defenders of French identity are so proud of? What is this universalism they claim to be protecting against the dominated groups' supposed 'communitarian tendencies'?

2) *Toward a true universalism*

This 'French model', which claims to be universalist, is in reality a false universalism.

It has erected the dominant gender as a model. This was easy enough when this was the only gender that mattered. In a second phase, when the dominated gender demanded a place for itself, it was told, 'Come on in, feel at ease just like in your . . . no, sorry, *my* own home'. So the dominated gender is required to conform to the model of the dominant. This is clearly impossible, because men are only men insofar as they exploit women. By definition, women cannot do what men do, 1) because they have no one to exploit; 2) because for women to become equal to men they would themselves have to stop being exploited; and 3) because if men no longer had women to exploit they would no longer be men. That is why women cannot be equal to what men are today, because 'what men are today' presupposes the subordination of women. The fear held by certain differentialist feminists – that equality would mean aligning women to the male model – is unfounded.[3]

This false universalism reproduces the structure of the gender system of which it is also a constituent part, notably in its juridical form. In this system, not only are the two genders unequal, but they stand in hierarchical relation: one of them positive, the other – by definition its opposite – negative. Moreover, these two genders do not play an equal role in defining humanity: women are specific whereas men are general; women are 'different' whereas men are simply 'normal'. That's normal enough; they are, of course, the norm. This vision of the world, gender ideology, impregnates all formal and informal institutions, starting with law. This worldview and the institutions that establish and embody it refuse women access to citizenship – and they do so in the name of the universal, that is, normality.

This model, which prevails across the majority of Western socio-juridical and political systems, is put forward as the basis for *equality between the sexes*: the model of formal equality. Formal equality, which ignores and fails to challenge patriarchal exploitation, results in a model that I call 'equity'. As we know, equity means whatever is just; and 'just' does not necessarily

---

3 Christine Delphy, 'Penser le genre: quels problèmes?'

48

mean 'equal'.[4] This philosophy, adopted by the French government in its submission to the 1995 World Conference on Women in Beijing, in effect tells women: 'Once you've done all the housework, and on condition that you have done so, you are entirely free to devote yourself to paid work. But don't expect to be paid as much as men, who are better able to concentrate on their careers. And since all this is going to be pretty tiring, we recommend that you only work part-time.' Equity does not put an end to the exploitation of women; it does not even recognize its existence. But it does allow women to pay their due in different ways: with more work or more money, or a combination of the two. It's exploitation à la carte.

And this formal equality, which brings us equity – meaning, a *just* inequality – is precisely what the partisans of French-style integration or republican universalism are defending. They propose to integrate the excluded, including women, by the sole means of rejecting explicit discrimination – which is to say, offering formal equality. On top of this, they oppose affirmative action as discriminatory, and insist that the mere lack of explicit discrimination is quite sufficient.

This counterposition between the absence of explicit discrimination, on the one hand, and affirmative action, on the other, implies that they are either dealing in sophistry, or plain confused. They are saying that in order to arrive at an equal society we have to act *as if* it already existed. Well, to act as if it were equal, when it isn't, is to perpetuate inequality. It means putting people who don't have the same resources on the same starting blocks, and then pretending to be surprised when they don't arrive at the finish line together.

Many liberals take offence at the fact that oppressed

---

4   Christine Delphy, 'Égalité, équivalence et équité: la position de l'État français au regard du droit international', *Nouvelles Questions féministes*, 16/1, 1995.

individuals form groups in order to overcome discrimination. But firstly, it is not the discriminated-against individuals who have made themselves into groups; rather, it is the people discriminating against them who have grouped and categorized them. Secondly, given that they are discriminated against for being members of these groups, it is only by fighting together that can they hope one day to be considered as individuals. But liberals would prefer that individuals oppressed for being members of a category (one specified by the dominant group) nonetheless present themselves at the beginning of the struggle as they would hope to be treated at its end – as individuals. This is a cut-price answer to the necessarily dialectical character of any struggle for inclusion in the universal – that is to say, the ability to be considered as a single individual and not as a woman, black, etc.

Women have common interests. Even if we define these interests in terms of the disappearance of gender categories, the achievement of this goal requires, in the first instance, women becoming conscious of this community of interests and thus uniting. The same goes for any dominated group that does not want to be dominated any more: to stop being a passive category, it must first constitute itself as an active political category. The quest to abolish gender categories does not at all stand in contradiction with the formation of political communities of gender – it would be absurd to say, 'In order to get somewhere, we need to pretend that we're already there'.

Universalism à la française targets dominated groups, suspecting them of harbouring communitarian or separatist goals. Yet by any logic universalism is not the opposite of communitarianism, but of particularism, in that it defends equal rights that are the same for everyone, as against rights for certain categories. Such universalism cannot exist – if women, or any other category, stand outside of common law. This is still the case for women in many fields: for example, the public/private divide is but the effective expression of the inequalities and differences in people's rights according to their sex and age[5] – if the subject of the common law – that is, a law that is meant to apply to everyone – is not really neutral or universal. And the implicit or explicit subject of law is man: this particular figure is supposed to embody the general populace. As we said earlier, he is normal and the norm.

Women will necessarily be at a disadvantage when it comes to meeting the demands of this norm and this common law, even in the absence of explicit discrimination and even if they are not subjected to special dispensations. Equal rights, true universalism, cannot be achieved unless we draw attention to the hidden specificity of the subject of universal rights. We must reveal his sexed, ethnicized and class nature, and replace this subject with an individual who could be any individual and who takes all individuals into account. The fact that in order to get compensation a woman has to prove that *a man* could have had the same illness – well, that's a version of equality that shows clearly enough what a fraud so-called formal equality is. The supposed universal has a *male referent* – not only in fact, but also in law.

The specificity of the legal subject will not disappear all by itself: it will only disappear if we actively work to eliminate it.

Conclusion
Universalism does not yet exist: it is a work in progress.[6] And its realisation requires a denunciation of false universalism:

---

5 Christine Delphy, 'L'état d'exception: la dérogation au droit commun comme fondement de la sphère privée', *Nouvelles Questions féministes*, 16/4, 1995.

6 Christine Delphy, 'Rapports de sexe, genre et universalisme', interview by Myriam Lévy and Patrick Silberstein, *Utopie critique*, 1995, 2.

for the principal obstacles to accomplishing universalism are those who pretend that it exists already. On the one hand, because they oppose the denunciation of false universalism; on the other hand, because in so doing – and this is, besides, their objective – they keep in place the pretend-universal common law such as it is. That is, they defend a particularist law whose reference point is the dominant subject, the white adult male. A rule that by definition disadvantages and excludes the dominated categories.

Moreover, we need to denounce the falsity of this universalism, because otherwise it is possible that these dominated categories, tired of being discriminated against systematically – that is, as an effect of the system – by what is meant to be universal law, will be tempted to establish similarly particularist rules of their own. Losing hope in finding justice within the common law, they may reject it and demand special dispensations. Ultimately, insofar as any such specific measures leave intact a common law that disadvantages the dominated, they will never bring these people true equality. The specific laws for women in France at the moment are detrimental to them, even when they seem to stand in their favour.[7]

Only in France does insistence on political participation take the form of the demand for parity, and seek a change in the law to this end. Elsewhere, lesser demands have been made and satisfied: for instance, quotas are the bread-and-butter of affirmative action in Scandinavia, where a committed policy at all levels of the state seeks to bring an end to the marginalization of half the population.

How can we not connect the apparent radicalism of this demand for parity to French society's tireless resistance to

---

7 Christine Delphy, 'L'état d'exception: la dérogation au droit commun comme fondement de la sphère privée', *Nouvelles Questions féministes*, 16/4, 1995.

abandoning the masculine as the norm, even at the level of language?[8] Is it any coincidence that this demand has emerged in France and not in Quebec, where women's presence in ministries, operating theatres and artists' studios is not hidden by 'masculine neuters'?[9]

How can we not connect this demand to the criminal decision made by the Constitutional Court, taking it upon itself to shut down the quotas proposal being discussed in the Parti Socialiste in 1982, indeed daring to condemn this on the basis that it would 'create categories within the Republic'? As if these categories did not exist anyway, had no judicial foundation, and were not in large part created by the law itself, in what it says as well as what it doesn't say.

How can we not connect (a) the insistent denial of women's oppression being disguised as the defence of universalism to (b) the fact that it's only in France that we have to justify women's participation in politics by way of differentialist arguments?

If the French version of universalism forbidding affirmative action forces women to get 'men' and 'women' written down in the constitution as two different species, then the dominants' diehard defence of their privileges will have had the paradoxical effect of transforming the fracture whose existence they so obstinately denied into a chasm. And just as bad money drives out the good, false universalism will have driven out true universalism.

---

8 Christine Delphy, 'Le baquelache en France', *Nouvelles Questions féministes*, 15/2, 1994.

9 Quebec law mandates the use of gender-neutral job titles, whereas the French typically use male-gendered terms – *translator's note.*

CHAPTER 3

Republican Humanitarianism Against Queer Movements

In the 'progressive' circles of the 1970s there were two complementary approaches to homosexuality. One was interpretative, defining homosexuality in the same terms as the dominant – psychoanalytic – theory, firstly as a sexual category and secondly as a sickness. The other, a political stance, was the so-called liberal position, declaring that we had to be tolerant of homosexuals, who, after all, didn't deliberately choose this condition and had already been punished enough by the mere fact of not having completed their psycho-sexual development, of having stopped halfway along. Stuck.

More to be pitied than blamed
This interpretation is still the same today. People who have had the bad luck to be born with incomplete software, lacking in particular the 'genital stage' programme, are the Peter Pans of the heart and the private parts, condemned to a life sentence of adolescence – that purgatory of Western culture. Forever children, without the advantage of innocence, condemned to playing with the wrong bits, joylessly hankering after the teacher and listening to Dalida[1] records, they will never reach emotional maturity – the private 'quiet strength'[2] – that a

---

1   A singer famous in France, particularly popular from the 1950s to 1980s – *translator's note.*

2   An amusing nod to 'Force tranquille' – a campaign slogan of French president François Mitterrand – *translator's note.*

55

heterosexual fuck brings, or even better, several of them (and that's not to mention missing out on the other sex's hormones, which are supplied for free, so to speak, in the exchange of fluids – we might compare it to taking vitamin pills).

All this was already known thirty years ago, at least among educated people, and this enlightened minority refused to lay any blame on homosexuals, who had to be considered a case of arrested growth, a pity for all concerned:[3] the homosexuals themselves, but also everyone else. A highly humanitarian position, of course, a credit to those who held it, then and now; and these enlightened souls haven't disappeared. As for the recipients of this generosity, well, they are changing, adopting a stance as old as human nature, alas: you give them an inch, and they take a mile. Who, them? Yeah, all of them! The faggots, the rail unions, the 'French of North African origin', other Arabs . . . women! . . . Even women! They want to have their cake and eat it: they want you to open the door for them and they also want to be paid as much as men! (We could mention in passing the problems that this demand causes for a number of men: a recent RATP report tells us that they would gladly give up 30 per cent of their wages each month in order not to have the door slammed in their face.)[4]

---

3   The spring 1971 public radio broadcast by Ménie Grégoire that MLF activists went along to heckle (during the 'Fête à Ménie') was entitled 'Homosexuality, this Sad Problem'. The Gouines rouges ['Red dykes'] Monique and Christine sang 'It's the Fête à Ménie, Ménie's dressed up nice, / Ménie's now a dyke, it's the Fête à Ménie', having composed these lines (to the tune of *La Java bleue*) in her honour. Also, they sang to another well-known tune, 'I'm in love with Ménie, / With her nice eyes, with her sociology, / And I often yearn for Ménie's view'. This was to the great amusement of the other feminists and the few boys we would soon have to drag along with us in the FHAR, created by Maryse and Anne-Marie not long afterwards.

4   The RATP did no research to back up this percentage; it was simply pulled out the air.

The queers, well, they're the same; they want to be queers *and* show it.

In these conditions it's unsurprising that the holders of the title 'genital adult', who know what they've been through to get it, call the queers to order; or, as one leader of the enlightened elite, Alain Finkielkraut,[5] put it so well, they ask for a little 'discretion'. Of course we wouldn't be a modern society if we didn't tolerate such handicaps – or rather, if we didn't do everything we could to alleviate their consequences. Social security,[6] reserved jobs, access ramps, free phone numbers, the Samaritans – we can't do enough to console their suffering. But there's a difference between a 'less hard' society – as requested by another humanitarian leader, Martine Aubry,[7] showing her wise moderation – and a world turned upside down (an 'entirely soft' one, perhaps?). But to be proud of your handicap is like saying that it's not a handicap at all. So what's the point of treading softly around it, like Finkielkraut? What is the point of going to all this bother to pretend we don't notice that the other is a queer, when the other tells us so himself?

We can't show our humanity to a handicapped person who refuses to recognize their handicap: if he wants to be treated in a humane way then he has to accept that he's handicapped – it's just common sense. It's clear that a society can only be humane if there are people we can be humane *to*. Just like how we need unemployed people if we want unemployment

---

5 Well-known French 'public intellectual' and self-professed left-winger. A reliable supporter of humanitarian interventions, Israeli foreign policy and the demonization of ethnic minorities – *translator's note*.

6 This has a broader meaning than the equivalent US term, including healthcare – *translator's note*.

7 A prominent figure in the Parti Socialiste, minister of social affairs at the time of writing in 1997. Mayor of Lille from 2001 onward, and from 2008 to 2012 First Secretary of this party – *translator's note*.

benefits, poor old people if we want a minimum pension, and housewives who can't take retirement if we want widows' pensions, etc. Humanity doesn't come to a society all by itself: everyone has to do their bit.

Solidarity [*solidarité*][8] has been adapted and modernized. The old image of solidarity was a group of people standing together – which, as everyone knows, is contrary to the 'convergence' criteria as decreed by the IMF and the World Bank. Today, when we think of 'solidarity' we think of an arm reaching out from up on high, pulling up a hand situated down below: much, much lower! That's how the person attached to the hand below gets out of the gutter. Or more exactly, does not fall into it but doesn't really get out of it either. Because if she did get out, then she wouldn't need solidarity any more – and then there'd be no more solidarity. The moment that best symbolizes solidarity appears in films sometimes, when someone's hanging off a cliff edge, gripping the end of someone's arm. That's where solidarity has to stop: holding someone in suspension.

Like any team sport, solidarity needs some to suspend and others to be suspended
Well, those categories of people that have traditionally been objects of opprobrium and simultaneously pity, who are thus the natural candidates for being suspended – women, Arabs, queers and others – have for some time been dragging their feet, when not straightforwardly refusing to play the game of solidarity.

As an example of this ill will we could look at the unity of gays and lesbians, starting twenty-seven years ago and

---

8   The French term *solidarité* has a broader meaning than 'solidarity', also including notions that in English would be described in terms of 'welfare' or 'charity' – *translator's note*.

continuing today. In varied forms: separately or together, for politics or for bike rides, or maybe both. Or always both, we might say. Because in getting together, whether to sing or to write to their representatives, gays and lesbians are doing something eminently political; whatever their analysis of society, and whatever their demands, they have made an enormous step. Being together? It seems basic. Yet it required a lot of taboos being broken. Living in squalor is one thing but seeking out the company of other sufferers is . . . morbid! We're told that we should at least hang around 'normal' people sometimes – it's for our own good, after all. But since 1970, with varying success but in growing numbers, queers have stopped trying to talk to people who can't or won't hear them mentioned, and have decided to start talking among themselves. And whether they say it or not, this talking among themselves says loud and clear that they don't consider themselves ill, but isolated. And when you understand that you're being isolated, you're not far from understanding that you're oppressed. After all, isolation is one of the great tools of oppression and the main factor in its continuation.

Let's talk about demands, then. At the beginning of the feminist and gay movements we denounced the family; now we want to be families. I have said what I think about civil partnership.[9] It is a shame that lesbians and gays have become blind or indifferent to the patriarchal character of marriage, demanding a contract for their own use based on the postulate that one of the two members of the couple is dependent on the other. But in another regard, I think that the civil partnership contract does have one quality that makes it a worthwhile proposition in the here and now, even if not entirely redeeming

---

9 Christine Delphy, 'Du contrat d'union civile, du mariage, du concubinage et de la personne, surtout féminine', *Nouvelles Questions féministes*, 2, 1992.

its faults: it encourages visibility. And visibility is precisely what society cannot tolerate. What did Finkielkraut say? 'Do what you will – but some discretion, please!'

This is a truly classic discourse, a seemingly anodyne and liberal one (and it is, indeed, liberal): after all, no one has to 'flaunt it'. And yet this is also what shows the lack of difference between the 'unenlightened', so-called homophobic position and the liberal one: this latter is no less repressive, it's just more hypocritical, that's all.

After all, in a society obsessed by 'sexual difference', which is always on the lookout for signs of conformity with the prescriptions of gender – judged maximal, adequate or insufficient – and obsessed by heterosexuality (and not sexuality, as we might imagine), then living without hiding night and day *necessarily* means 'flaunting' your homosexuality. There is no half-measure or middle or neutral position, any more than there is a third sex. Either you 'pass' – as heterosexual – or else people start 'asking questions' and end up finding answers. Discretion is a double life: clandestinity in peacetime. But is there any peace for women or queers, who are constantly on alert, constantly in danger? In danger of being 'unmasked' when they try to 'pass'; ostracized, discriminated against or even assaulted. And as everyone knows, no one hides when they have nothing to be ashamed of; so the queers themselves come to think that they're doing something wrong. Discretion also means listening to your colleagues or to the stories of your fellow diners and keeping your own mouth shut, never talking about yourself. It means being alone. It means lying. A little, a lot, actively or by what you don't say. Even to your own friends. Your self-esteem can't withstand being treated like this for long. To live in fear, to live a lie, to be alone and hold yourself in disdain: that's what the liberals force on us when they *only* ask for discretion.

Gay movements didn't play the liberals' game. Firstly – we

told them – because we no longer needed to do so. The same was true for women's movements. In 1970 when the feminist movement was created, they asked us why it was necessary: the liberal-experts-on-the-oppression-of-others told us that everything was already sorted, and there was nothing – really, nothing – left to demand. In 1997 they're coming out with all the same stuff: they tell us that women today 'have it all'. *Before*, oh, yes, then feminism *was* necessary; though curiously enough they now locate this 'before' back in 1970, when . . . etc., etc.

So gay movements are no use at all – they might have been useful back when they didn't exist, but today, now that 'homophobia has disappeared' . . . Well, it's gone away. What way did it go? I don't know. But in any case it's not around anymore, so you can see that you've no business here. Come on, move along now, please. It is amusing to watch the discrepancies in experts' and social movements' timing. If you listen to the experts, social movements are never in the right place at the right time or in the right form. Doubtless they've seen so many that they've become jaded. Touraine, for example, was rather picky when it came to the December 1995 strike movement.[10] It wasn't a real social movement, you see. He had already refused to give his approval to the women's movement: 'they didn't understand who the real enemy was'. As for December 1995, it was a 'corporatist movement of the already-privileged' (the new term for railworkers, it seems). He rejected them, too. A harsh judgement. Though not as harsh as the experts' judgement on the gay and lesbian movements. These really trouble the experts on universalism,

---

10   Millions-strong strike against pay freezes and pension 'reforms' in the public sector, including impressive participation by railworkers whose right to retire at fifty-five was under threat. The Juppé government abandoned most of its plans in the face of the strike – *translator's note*.

civilization and everything else. They think it presents a great danger. Firstly, for us: the risk of ghettoization. And they remind us that the ill-fated central European Jews' mania for building ghettos and holing up in them – rather than coming out for a drink with everyone else, downing a few vodkas and cracking some anti-Semitic jokes – only brought them pogroms. The Slavs are a proud race; you can't turn your nose up at them with impunity. And it's nice to have these specialist historians helping us out. Then (more seriously?) they pose the question: why do that lot, who have nothing left to ask for, still hang around together? Some sort of plot, it must be. Against whom? Well, against the Republic, that's it. Homos banding together is com-mu-ni-tar-i-an-is-m, nothing more, nothing less. No one knows exactly what that is, of course – political terms that are vague and full of threats are all the more terrible for their lack of specificity. We fear the worst.

A gay homeland in Ariège, perhaps?

This hysteria is surprising, and the pretext for it even more so. Real communitarianism means the coexistence of different rules for different parts of the population, described as communities. That is the case in Lebanon where Druzes have a different civil law than the Maronites, and in turn theirs is different than the Muslims'. That is the case in Israel and in India (among other places), where 'personal status codes' regulate marriage, inheritance, etc. according to people's religious affiliation. As far as I'm aware, that's not what gay movements are asking for, here or anywhere else. In fact, they're demanding exactly the *opposite*: they want the *common* law to be applied to them equally, and the abrogation of the exceptions and exemptions that make them into a specific category. The present situation is the real communitarianism: not *theirs*, but the communitarianism of the society that discriminates against them. And they want an end to this situation.

The 'communitarian' reproach is so ill-founded and the accusations of 'plotting against national unity' so grotesque that we must ask what they are a cover for. We see the real content of 'liberalism on moral questions' in the anger that grips the humanitarian-liberals when we unite: a rage that is very real.

The movements irritate them because we no longer appear before the representatives of the hetero-patriarchal order as atomized individuals. And the beauty of this formidable, pervasive order is that it can be represented by any of its 'Lacombe Luciens'.[11] That is why they wanted – and still want – us to be *alone*. To have us all for themselves. When we followed their sadistic lovers' rules – don't see anyone, don't talk to anyone, wait for me to call; when we were disoriented by their contradictory instructions, lost as we hurried from one hiding place to another and dazed by the lies – theirs as well as ours; when panicked about being alone; well, then we fell into their arms, ill, just as they always said we were. And thus they could deploy their 'humanity', their 'solidarity', with us on the receiving end. We were *suspended* from their lips offering words of compassion, *suspended* from their hands prescribing valium, and *suspended* from their understanding and tolerance; *suspended* on their conditions.

The hangman was the carer, the carer was the aggressor. That's the reality of liberalism, which adopts the disguise of republican universalism (a.k.a. humanitarian liberalism or liberal humanitarianism), or else takes better-known forms: the abusive parent, the possessive lover, the stalker or the violent husband. The pimp is the archetype of this figure. Who strikes and consoles, consoles and strikes. The figure of omnipotence: a role hard to give up.

---

11   The titular character of 1974's *Lacombe Lucien*, a film about a young Gestapo collaborator in Vichy France who falls in love with a Jewish girl – *translator's note*.

And yet, it'll have to happen. The liberals will have to give it up. When they mock gay 'pride' – 'Proud of what, dear god?' – their laughter is forced. Because they know that this system can only work if they force us to lead an objectively shameful way of life, such that we become paralysed by a subjective shame that leaves us at the mercy of our enemies. They know that washing off the shame means wiping away the paralysis: that we will answer their humanitarianism with solidarity among equals. And that the movements – feminists, queers and the rest, including the ones that don't exist yet – will not disappear. We will not be suspended any longer.

CHAPTER 4

A War Without End

The United States has gone to war.

All European countries support it, in principle at least. The war's stated objective of 'eradicating terrorism' is absurd: for there is not *one* terrorism, but *several*. The chosen strategy is suicidal. We must demand that our government try to stop the coming crimes, and if that does not succeed, then we must at least abstain from participating.

How have we come to this? Agreeing to participate in a war that endangers all of us? The conditioning of public opinion started with the efforts to play on people's sense of compassion: everything possible was done to manipulate our emotions, and the United States became so central to our everyday existence that we even came to think that we were Americans. Added to this, all the articles on the 9/11 attacks follow the same compulsory order. The first part, 'It's horrible', establishes the incomparable magnitude of the catastrophe (indeed, without comparing it to anything else at all, except perhaps Pearl Harbor) and the martyrdom of the victims, which is also held to be incomparable. The second part, 'It's incomprehensible', repeats *ad infinitum* that these attacks can only be explained by the monstrousness of their authors, the demonization of the suicide bombers being one way of denying that these attacks have any causes. The American media generally stop at that. Their European counterparts add a short rider to this, a 'This makes me think', standing in total contradiction to what went before, where it says as if in passing that America's response will leave 'the fundamental problems' unresolved.

And when these problems are specified, they always revolve around the US's favouritism toward Israel and the sanctions against Iraq.

So there certainly are causes. And not causes that could be declared 'irrelevant' just because terrorists are raising these issues. But since these terrorists left no explanation, and no one has claimed responsibility nor posed any demands, what we have here are the causes sought out and identified as pertinent and valid by Westerners themselves. But even so, the press refuses to give them the place they deserve as explanations. Because to do so would require getting rid of the section 'It's incomprehensible'. And this section is essential for what comes next – namely, the decision to go to war. The media have told us enough times that the victims were innocent. Of course they are, like all victims of armed terrorist groups or of the state terrorism for which the US is mainly if not solely responsible. It is estimated that the direct military interventions and coups organized by the United States since the end of the Second World War have killed around eight million people in over twenty countries. So why this superfluous repetition of the words 'innocent victims'? It expresses what everyone thinks, but what can't be said: that an American life is worth dozens, hundreds or even thousands of other lives (*The Independent* of 21 September estimated that the exchange rate of global suffering, as measured by the US media, currently stands at 100,000 Rwandans to twelve American schoolkids.) In the 'It's incomprehensible' section we can also find the words 'folly' or 'murderous folly' every two lines. Naturally enough – for we can hardly expect to understand the mad. To avoid having to listen to someone we can always just label them crazy.

Not only the Bush administration but also the American and European media decided without a second thought that war was the answer. In order to justify the war, they had to pretend not to know any of the reasons behind the hatred of the United States that tens of millions of people feel the world over. This is what all the media did, heaping blame on 'anti-Americanism' – an individual attitude coming from God knows where, a quasi-pathological view lacking any objective foundation. Indeed, to recognize that we know the reasons behind this resentment would have meant recognizing that however wrong we think they are, these are human reasons expressed by human beings, with whom discussion is possible, indeed indispensable if we want a truly collective, global order.

At the same time, however, in changing its policy a little – '[Bush] himself picked up the phone to get a ceasefire from Ariel Sharon' (*Le Monde*, 24 September 2001) – the United States showed that it knows that the terrorists didn't act 'gratuitously', and that American policy does lead to rational grievances. But we can predict that this pressure on Israel will remain an exceptional case. The US knows, but denies that it knows: 'It is extremely important that the leaders of Europe and the United States make it understood that these attacks have nothing to do with the Middle East peace process': James Rubin, advisor to Madeleine Albright, *Le Monde*, 27 September 2001.

Indeed, admitting that they know the causes of these attacks would almost mean admitting that it is necessary to find remedies to them. Well, in immediately opting for war, the US government announced that it had no intention of changing its policy in any way; on the contrary, it wanted to amplify its 'unilateral' character, that is, an autistic policy operating outside of international law. The NATO countries that had taken something of a distance from US policy, badgering the US about its debts to the UN or its rejection of the Kyoto Protocol, were called to order. They fell back into line without a fuss. The West closed ranks, forgetting in the blink of an eye its declarations of solidarity with the Third World.

The state of states, the United States, today demands no less than a monopoly on legitimate international violence. Indeed, what will be left of international law and the UN's prerogatives, now that whoever is not 'with' the United States is 'against' it, and thus exposed to its anger? What will be left of the rule of law if we hunt Bin Laden 'dead or alive' without providing proof of his guilt, when we know that in the past attacks blamed on Islamists proved to come from a quite different quarter (as in Oklahoma City)? Some are betting on the emergence of a less unipolar world order, since the US will need partners in the fight against 'terrorism'. But who can believe in a revival of international negotiations amid such an unbalanced situation, in which the United States unilaterally takes recourse to military might? What would the negotiations lead to? Using the opening provided by these attacks, the United States wants to consolidate the 'New World Order' it brought into being with the first Gulf War, as well as with the decline of the UN, whose Security Council in 1991 became a kind of recording studio for the decisions America had already made.

Today, the message that the US sends to all countries – those whose support it demands as well as those that it threatens – is 'Not only will we not recognize what we have done wrong, not only will we not stop overthrowing governments, starving peoples, and bombing civilians where we want and when we want, for our own reasons, which we don't have to explain to anyone – but you're going to resign yourselves to it, and even applaud'. Today they want the whole world to recognize what their strength has *de facto* allowed them to do for decades *as their right*. Exceptional. Divine. Infinite.

The women and men of this country must reject this demand, as exorbitant as it is cynical, refusing to be accomplices in the massacres now being prepared. Rather, we must concentrate our fire on the causes of the current situation, instead of pretending that military destruction will allow us to eliminate the despair that we should have taken as a warning. In less than a week the Bush administration has freed up $40 billion for the war, which represents half the amount it would take to eradicate malnutrition and guarantee the *whole world population* access to clean water and basic healthcare (UNDP report, 1994). These sums should be devoted to the development of Afghanistan and more generally the cancelling of the debts of poor countries; and the foreign policy of the great powers should finally respect the principles proclaimed in international conventions and declarations, so as to cut the roots of future hatred. That's the way to guarantee security for all – not with yet more arrogance and yet more bombs. Many have already spoken this self-evident truth: beginning a holy war against Afghanistan – and in the process instrumentalizing the cause of women, which *all* the protagonists disdain equally – means creating a bloc of states and individuals that support the United States, and it thus will unleash a cycle of reprisals as old as terrorism itself, hurting and destabilizing all countries. This is just opening Pandora's box.

First and foremost, it is urgently important that we reject any French participation in this adventure and that we form an international coalition against the project now taking shape: namely, the North's war without end against the South.[1]

---

1   This article was written in collaboration with Jacques Bidet, Danièle Kergoat, Willy Pelletier and Jacques Texier.

CHAPTER 5

Guantánamo and the
Destruction of the Law

Since the beginning of the American military action in Afghanistan, indeed, since the attacks against the Twin Towers, we have seen a rapid debasement of the law. Not so much the application of law, which so often leaves much to be desired, especially in times of war; but the recognition of the principles at the basis of law, and even the recognition that principles are necessary.

On the one hand, new security measures that supposedly help the struggle against terrorism are everywhere imperilling the civil liberties that each nation's laws once guaranteed. On the other hand, international law has been trampled on – by Israel for decades, and by the United States since the first Gulf War (January 1991) and above all since September 2001.

The United States is not the first country to violate international law; what is new is that the US no longer seeks to make any excuses for this; on the contrary, it defies the very principles of international law, openly saying that it doesn't see the need for them. What is even newer, and graver still, is that it does not challenge these principles in order to replace them with other, different ones, as in the case of civil liberties. No. When it comes to international law, and more particularly the laws of war, at the very moment that the United States supports the judgment against Milošević at International Criminal Court's tribunal for Yugoslavia, it openly declares that it considers all such rules too much of a burden on its own plans.

If the Guantánamo Bay situation is an exemplary case, this is not because the fate of the prisoners incarcerated there is the most horrible that exists. Other detainees are sent to countries that practise torture; since 9/11 still others have secretly been locked away in US prisons, without lawyers, without us even knowing their names. Even the numbers are vague: people say there's two thousand, or six hundred, or three hundred of them. Their only crime is to be of Arab origin or Muslim faith. We emphasize the Guantánamo case because the American administration has not shied away from talking about and photographing it; and on the basis of these images and statements, human rights NGOs have been able to denounce the conditions in which the detainees are held as well as the US government's transgression of international law.

The treatment of the Guantánamo Bay prisoners is an illustration – though it's not the only one – of the risk we run in accepting Bush's notion of terrorism and the war against terrorism without any kind of due process. And yet all governments have accepted it, some of them enthusiastically so: and we can now see how this allows for each and every situation to be defined as 'unprecedented', with all existing laws dismissed as no longer relevant. Of course, the danger resides not in the word 'terrorism' itself but in its use: before, there were terrorist actions that could be dealt with in terms of ordinary criminal law. But now there are terrorist individuals, and according to the US administration, the mere attribution of this label strips them of any rights, even the minimal rights that we recognize even in the case of the worst criminals. And to be considered a terrorist you don't necessarily have to have committed a terrorist act, nor even any crime at all: it is enough that you were arrested during the course of the 'struggle against terrorism'.

The treatment of the Guantánamo Bay prisoners provides a striking example – though it's not the only one – of the winners setting the rules. The laws of war were an advance over ancient Rome's *vae victis* – meaning that the defeated could not expect any justice from their conquerors, that they had no rights, and in short that their defeat deprived them of their human status. In fact, Rome did not recognize this status in any case, seeing only its own citizens as subjects of law. The laws of war succeeded in restoring the humanity of the defeated, at least in principle. But in the space of a few weeks, even before Guantánamo, the US turned back the clock – and it did so in two steps. Firstly, through a 23 November 2001 presidential decree creating military tribunals; and this was a truly Roman decision, because these tribunals are exclusively reserved for foreigners, for those who are not American citizens. Secondly, with the treatment of the Guantánamo prisoners and the arguments that the American authorities used to justify it.

The dehumanization of the enemy, a prelude to the establishment of arbitrary rule

The treatment of the Guantánamo prisoners, characterized as 'terrorists' without any evidence being presented, marked a major regression: the abandonment of *habeas corpus*, that great principle of Western law otherwise known as the presumption of innocence. This move, a break with the very basis of our rights, does, however, stand in continuity with the racist practices springing from colonialism. This continuity is blatantly obvious in the use of double standards, fundamentally similar to those used in other circumstances, according to which white lives are worth more than brown ones. The victims of the New York attacks have the right to flowers and wreaths, speeches and ceremonies, but also and above all, a name, a photo, an individual biography recorded in the newspapers; the Afghan victims of the American bombs are invisible and anonymous, and not even roughly counted. Israeli civilians are always mentioned first in the media: we are always told that they've been murdered by terrorists, whereas the Palestinian civilians 'die during Israeli incursions'. No human agency was involved in their death; there were no murderers, it was just a coincidence that they died at the same time as the incursions took place.

So what's new here? What's new is that this time the racism is spoken and openly asserted, formalized and institutionalized in criminal law. Before, this wasn't the case.

While the law is meant to be the same for everyone, this is not true in civil law that recognizes categories of citizens. But in most countries criminal law is in principle the same for everyone when it comes to common law crimes; its application may be different if excuses can be made – the plaintiff is insane or a minor – but a crime is a crime, no matter who commits it. So criminal law has long been the same for both sexes, while civil law was different for women and for men. Foreigners who have committed a crime in a given country are judged as its own citizens would be: this principle has always been a commonplace. But with the creation of specific tribunals for foreigners, the United States has overthrown the universally accepted principle that a crime is judged according to the law of the country, not the nationality of its perpetrator. The United States has thus established in principle what was previously considered a discriminatory practice, which could be denounced and condemned precisely because it was an infamy against the law.

The treatment of the Guantánamo prisoners has not created the scandal that it ought to, because Western public opinion – to a significant degree imbued with racism, be it overt or implicit – has accepted their demonization without any difficulty. Some will say that the enemy is treated like this in any war. Indeed, during the First World War, French propaganda featured cartoons showing German soldiers cutting off

French children's hands. But this representation of 'monsters' was at odds with the ordinary representation of Germans – even when it was pejorative or mocking – who were fundamentally considered an equal neighbour. The demonization of the Guantánamo prisoners, conversely, stands in perfect continuity with the representation of Arabs and Third World people in general as inferior, as savages, in short, as *untermensch*, sub-humans. Since they are not fully human, they are not far from being animals. In turn, the best way of proving what we know already – that they're not people like we are – is to present them as animals. That is what they've done at Guantánamo. To set them beyond the law it is first necessary to place them completely outside of humanity. Hence the ski masks to cover up their eyes and the muzzles to stop them from speaking. These muzzles are justified by invoking the fear that the prisoners might bite someone. What better way to say that these are not men, but dogs – rabid dogs? Finally, their feet and wrists are chained up – they are shackled to cages and watched over by guards twenty-four hours a day. These are wild animals, and the proof that they're wild animals is that they've been put in cages.

This total dehumanization would be impossible without the element of racism. In turn, it provides a formal legal grounding for entire groups of people to be treated in a totally different way: and these are racial and cultural categories, namely Arabs and Muslims. These groups, already the victims of racism for multiple historical reasons – the French colonization of North Africa, the British and French 'mandates', and the Israelis taking over from the British in Palestine – are now officially designated as criminals. Thus all Arabs and all Muslims become terrorist suspects, and within the terms of America's new rules, a suspected terrorist is already a criminal. Indeed, the new practices – some of them illegal, like the internment of foreigners; others partly legal, like tribunals for foreigners – have wiped away the distinction between someone who is merely a 'suspect' and someone who is 'guilty' in the United States. This legalized discriminatory treatment can only reinforce spontaneous racism, deepening the divide of hatred and distrust between the West and the rest of the world.

Internment at Guantánamo is contrary to international and criminal law

The Guantánamo prisoners were transported there from Afghanistan on 11 January 2002. They were then held in conditions that can only be described as arbitrary incarceration, which the FDIH [International Human Rights Federation] has already denounced. As yet they have not been charged with anything: they are not being held in jail until their trials begin, but simply being held. This detainment will last longer than any previously known legal procedure, and without any of the usual guarantees: phone calls, a lawyer, etc. The Americans say that their detention (as unlimited as the war on terrorism itself) could continue indefinitely. The only possible justification for their detention without having been charged would be if they were considered prisoners of war. But again, according to the Geneva Convention such a condition would only apply up until the close of hostilities. The magistrates' union considers that this date has already passed, declaring on 20 March 2002 that 'The mere fact of having taken part in combat cannot justify their internment unless it has been proven that they are guilty of war crimes, genocide or crimes against humanity, incriminated in the statutes of the International Criminal Court. According to Article 118 of the Geneva Convention they must be released and repatriated without delay after the end of active hostilities.'

The United States denies them the status of prisoners of war, in spite of the protests made by groups of lawyers, the International Federation for Human Rights, Human Rights

Watch, Amnesty International and, recently, by the human rights commission of the Organization of American States. The Geneva Convention stipulates that all people taken prisoner on the battlefield must be treated as POWs. They have the right to the exact same treatment as the armed forces of the country jailing them. If there is some remaining doubt as to the person's POW status, then this is a matter for a tribunal to decide. If the tribunal refuses to attribute them POW status, then the detainees still benefit from the protections of the fourth Geneva Convention, concerning civilians arrested during the course of a conflict.

Even if civilians do not have the right to be treated as POWs, this fourth convention formally prohibits their removal from the place where they were arrested – in the case of the Guantánamo prisoners, it prohibits their deportation from Afghanistan to Guantánamo Bay. It's notable that no NGO has used this convention as its basis for denouncing the US's deportation of people arrested in Afghanistan to Guantánamo, which is veritable kidnapping. By constrast, NGOs have waged a valiant struggle to demand that the detainees be treated as POWs, and have vigorously opposed the new military tribunals. They have not had much success. The US administration has agreed to apply the Geneva Convention to Taliban prisoners, but not to al-Qaeda members, while also insisting that it needs a lot of time in order to distinguish between the two. Moreover, the US persists in refusing POW status to its detainees, even to Taliban soldiers. They are still being hauled in front of the new military tribunals, whose summary rulings have been slightly modified in response to protests, now allowing the possibility of public trials and the right of appeal. Even so, they are still a legal killing machine, the decision in the last instance remaining the American president's sovereign prerogative.

The US will need a lot of time to organize these trials, since it's 'difficult to prepare the indictments', as the American Secretary of Defense Donald Rumsfeld declared on 21 March 2002. While they wait for that, the prisoners – who are not even suspects in the usual sense, since they have not been charged – have no right to family visits or lawyers. Recently, a further announcement swept away what remained of rights that we might still have believed untouchable. Rumsfeld declared that even in the event that these far-off trials ended in acquittals, the prisoners would not be released. 'These are dangerous people, we can't let them back out on the streets, it's just common sense', he told us.

The demolition of all the foundations of law, and the rest of the world's silence

Some of the detainees are nationals of European countries. While Sweden demanded the repatriation of a prisoner with Swedish citizenship, the other governments, notably Great Britain and France, did not exercise their duty to protect their own nationals. France has already sent four missions to Guantánamo: but it's clear that the purpose of these missions was to gather information for the French police – members of the intelligence services took part in these trips – and to help their American counterparts, not to defend the rights of the Frenchmen held captive there. At the end of the third mission, on 2 April 2002, the Quai d'Orsay [French Foreign Office] spokesman made a striking statement. When asked, 'Do we know what the allegations are?', he replied, 'That was not the objective of this mission.' And when asked, 'Have you offered legal support?' he explained, 'We did not address that point, it was not the objective of our visit.' And again when asked, 'Do you know what they are accused of?' he answered, 'No.'

So the European countries totally capitulated in the face of the arbitrary rule establishment by United States; these countries violated their own laws by refusing their citizens normal diplomatic protection and leaving them in the hands of illegal entities like the Guantánamo camp. But they also violated international law: every state that signs the Geneva Convention is obliged to make other states respect it, too. Yet far from pulling the United States back onto the right track, the European countries pretended not to notice the blatant illegality of these practices.

In the 'struggle against terrorism', the Geneva Convention and other instruments of international law, already routinely violated by other countries – for example, Israel's many years of deporting people from the territories that it occupies and waging war on civilians, without anyone reminding it that this is forbidden by the fourth Geneva Convention – have now been declared null and void by the United States. A country, that is, which claims to determine its relations with other states according to how much respect they show for human rights . ... Law itself is shackled. All this sweeps aside the distinctions between a suspect – a person who is interrogated without being charged; a defendant – a person charged with a crime and defending themselves; and a criminal – someone who has been judged by due process and found guilty. And without these distinctions, justice itself collapses. The denial of justice is even expressed in the questions (however well intentioned) that journalists pose to the Quai d'Orsay [French Foreign Office]: 'Would the detainees prefer to be *tried* in France?' – forgetting, in the process, that you can't be tried when you haven't even been charged. That journalists can forget this so easily tells us something about the drift that is taking place, but also about the mediocrity with which they do their jobs. When they ask, 'What are they accused of?', they assume that the prisoners have been accused of anything at all. But based on Rumsfeld's comment that 'it's difficult to prepare the indictments', as well as on informal information given to some of the French detainees' lawyers, it turns out that they have *not* been charged. So they are being held in custody arbitrarily, after having been transported out of Afghanistan illegally.

Freedom under threat

No government – and no French media outlet – has commented on Rumsfeld's truly amazing statement, the icing on the cake of the systematic destruction of law. If you're not released even when you're acquitted, what's the difference between being innocent and guilty? The very purpose of criminal law vanishes. So why bother with the indictment, the ministry of justice, the defence, the trial, the jury, and so on, as in the past? José Padilla, suspected of preparing a 'dirty' bomb and arrested on 8 May in Chicago after arriving from Switzerland, had to appear before a jury. After a little sleight of hand, he was rebaptized as an 'enemy combatant' and – hey presto! – no more lawyer and no more trial, as he headed for indefinite secret detention. Yet there was no bomb: he was just suspected of having wanted to make it.

Few people or political groups outside of legal circles seem to be aware of the grave seriousness of these new American doctrines and practices. Perhaps some still see law as a 'super-structure', if not a bourgeois mystification, even when everyone's freedom is under threat (who can be sure of not ending up like José Padilla, the latest victim of this state of exception that has now become the norm?), even when the logic of this arbitrary rule over individuals is the same arbitrary rule over peoples that allows the United States to destroy whatever country is unlucky enough to displease it – whether by dropping its bombs, fomenting coups d'état or imposing embargos. It is the logic of a state drunk on its own power: a literally untrammelled power. Free of any constraints, American power believes that it stands above the law, when in reality it is an *outlaw*.

CHAPTER 6

A War for Afghan Women?

Since the capture of Kabul it seems that the coalition against
terrorism has turned the war in Afghanistan over to the liberation of Afghan women. In his 29 January 2002 State of the
Union address, George W. Bush declared: 'The American flag
flies again over our embassy in Kabul . . . today women are
free.' But if we think back to the order of events, this must be
the fourth change of objective since the war began. On 11
September 2001 Bush declared war on no one in particular and
the world in general. This did correspond to the reality; but it
was rather too much of an innovation for the press and public
for him to be able to keep it up. So the next day a specific
enemy came into view: Bin Laden, whom the United States
called on the Taliban to hand over. To them, the Americans.
Faced with the Taliban's response – a typical one in extradition
cases – demanding proof of Bin Laden's guilt, the United
States repeated its ultimatum. Two weeks later it rejected the
Taliban's fresh offer to hand Bin Laden over to a neutral
country: it called this proposal 'negotiations', and by God,
how the United States doesn't like to negotiate.[1]

---

[1] On 22 September the Taliban offered to hand over Bin Laden if the
US could produce evidence against him – which it refused to do. But on 1
October, Mullah Omar suggested that Bin Laden be extradited to Pakistan,
where he could be kept under house arrest in Peshawar until he appeared
before an international tribunal, and this even without any proof being
given. The United States disdainfully rejected this offer, reiterating what
White House spokesman Ari Fleischer had often stated, 'There will be no
discussions or negotiations with the Taliban.' If war was the only solution,

81

'Smiling at you from Kabul'

Following this, Defense Secretary Rumsfeld told us that Bin Laden would perhaps never be found: and a third objective appeared; for now the Taliban regime itself was the enemy. There was no lack of arguments against the regime. I would go further: these arguments existed six years ago, and for six years they had not been a reason to go to war. Yet suddenly they did suffice. Not all by themselves, of course: as well as being odious, the Taliban harboured Bin Laden, suspected of being the author of the 9/11 attacks. After a month of bombing, the Allied troops entered Kabul, and the West declared victory, believing that they'd done a fine thing at little cost. The papers published pictures of smiling women – sorry, I mean, the smile of one woman – and the war found its fourth objective: the liberation of women. The fourth but perhaps not the last – for that, it would have to prove to be the 'right' reason.

And it turns out that it isn't the right one. For the people who the 'Allies against terrorism'[2] have brought to power are no better than the Taliban. We can no longer pretend that the Northern Alliance is something it's not. And given the number of reporters 'on the ground', it won't be possible to hide for much longer the contempt that the people of Kabul and Jalalabad feel toward their new rulers.[3] Indeed, this disdain is born of their own experience: between 1992 and 1996 the Northern Alliance's troops perpetrated massacres and

---

this was because the United States had no interest in anything else: they ruled out the alternative of diplomacy in advance, even when their enemies were asking for it (see the site Women living under Muslim Laws: www. wluml.org).

2   All those states whose rhetoric was in line with the United States; the US prosecuted the war by itself, however.

3   Patrice Claude, 'Le pouvoir désordonné des moudjahidins s'installe sur Jalalabad en proie à toutes les terreurs', *Le Monde*, 25–26 November 2001.

gratuitous killings of prisoners and the wounded, terrorizing civilians and robbing them blind. We cannot pretend that what happened in those years is not now happening again, in almost identical fashion, in an Afghanistan again being divided up into fiefdoms. Indeed, the revived warlordism only promises a return to the multiple civil wars that devastated the country between the Soviets leaving and the Taliban coming to power.

Taliban and the mujahideen: six of one, half a dozen of the other

It's not the right reason because the United States is not the friend of Afghan women. Women's rights have never been the US's concern – no more so in Afghanistan than in Kuwait or Saudi Arabia or anywhere else. We could even say that the opposite is true, and that the United States knowingly and voluntarily sacrificed Afghan women on the altar of American interests. How far do the mujahideen (the current manifestation of which is called the Northern Alliance) go back? Even before the Soviet army invaded the country in 1979 to replace one Marxist president (Hafizullah Amin) with another (Babrak Karmal), the tribal chiefs and religious authorities declared holy war on the Marxist leadership of Nur Mohammed Taraki.[4] Even before the struggle against the foreign invasion began, in 1978 the Khans and the mullahs took up arms against a government that forced girls to go to school and forbade levirate marriage and the sale of women. That is what shocked, scandalized and repulsed them. Yes, they do see women's rights as worth fighting over: worth fighting *against*. They became mujahideens: soldiers of God, against impious Marxism. The Soviet invasion gave this struggle a patriotic dimension. The Americans helped the mujahideens, since their enemies' enemies were their friends, no matter what they

---

4   Ahmed Rashid, *Taliban*, London: Pan, 2001.

wanted or did. Of course the United States did know what the mujahideens wanted: to pull women back into line. But they were against Moscow, and that was all that counted as far as the United States was concerned. Alas, this was also all that mattered in the eyes of the quixotic, pioneering 'French Doctors',[5] for whom 'anti-Soviet' was synonymous with 'freedom fighter'. Whose freedom? They didn't even think about that: they found the mujahideens' turbans rather fetching, and the adventure was all rather exciting. Do-gooding surrounded by magnificent scenery, while also helping the struggle against totalitarianism: what more could any young Western man have asked for? As for women's rights: for God's sake, these are their customs, and customs are sacred – particularly if you don't have to suffer them personally.[6]

The media's whitewashing of the Western coalition's mercenaries

In 1988 the Soviet army withdrew. The mujahideens' only remaining enemy was the government of Najibullah, the country's final Marxist prime minister. The mujahideens all fought in the name of Islam, for an Islamic state and for the application of sharia law: hence their name. In Pashto, Urdu and all the other local languages they are called *jihadis*, which is obviously enough derived from *jihad*. They never made any secret of their fundamentalism. Nonetheless, during the war against the Soviets, the French pretended to believe that this name meant 'freedom fighters'. And French TV was even more overcome with disinformation following the 'events' of 9/11. In September 2001 it showed the hagiographical film *Massoud l'Afghan*,[7] as

---

5 Generic name for French-based humanitarian organizations, from Médecins sans Frontières to Médecins du monde, etc.

6 See *Massoud l'Afghan* in the next paragraph.

7 A film by Christophe de Ponfilly that irresponsibly idealized its subject – if it was not a deliberate work of disinformation, that is.

well as a documentary made by unnamed Afghan women who used a hidden camera to film executions carried out by the Taliban in a Kabul football stadium. After the fall of Kabul some information on the behaviour of the 'allied' troops did begin to filter through. But clearly the French media censored themselves, thus denying the public objective and balanced coverage. They had no lack of sources: even though their own knowledge of the region is paltry – no French newspaper has a permanent correspondent in Pakistan – they could have made recourse to foreign press agencies, papers, TV stations and websites. But they deliberately hid this information under a bushel, refusing to look at the articles that we (the Coalition internationale contre la guerre) sent them. We had to wait until 23 January 2002 before the film on the Kabul stadium executions was reshown in full (on the TV station Arte) in Saira Shah's *Sorties de ténèbres?*; before we learned that it had been produced by the women of RAWA (the Revolutionary Association of the Women of Afghanistan);[8] and before another documentary, Antonia Rados's *Femmes de Kaboul* (also produced thanks to RAWA) showed the reality of women's lives after the so-called liberation, leaving it to the Afghans to explain what the journalists had been hiding for four months: namely, that the repression of women began with the mujahideens, and not with Taliban rule.

Recently, *Télérama* broke with the politically correct consensus, interviewing an Afghan musician who said, 'When the communists came to power in 1979 the possibilities for

---

8 RAWA's activists have for years been working among Afghan refugees in Pakistan, operating underground, and particularly focusing on the education of girls. They also enter into Afghanistan, indeed risking their lives to make films on the country's situation under the Taliban. Under the shadow of fundamentalist death threats, they attack the mujahideens just as they attack the Taliban; and they relentlessly opposed the US bombing of their country.

performing multiplied, and I could even go and do music classes in girls' schools . . . The problems began with the arrival of the mujahideens in 1992.'⁹ Holding back information might seem anodyne, but it is one of the principal mechanisms used to shape public opinion. On the one hand, the Western powers could not admit that they were standing shoulder-to-shoulder with such dubious forces; since the muja- hideens were the Western coalition's allies, 'We have so idolized these gunmen . . . that we are now immune to their history.'¹⁰ On the other hand, in order to justify their war in the eyes of public opinion, they had to promise that it would bring some 'improvement' in the Afghans' situation, and not only American vengeance or the consolidation of Western power. And public opinion wouldn't have believed in the promised improvements if it knew the truth about the Northern Alliance. So not only through the shameful lies of habitual propagan- dists like Bernard-Henri Lévy, but also and above all through what they omitted to mention, the Western powers counter- posed the 'bad' Taliban to the 'good' mujahideens – at least up until the point of the latter's victory.

Why the Taliban came to power in 1996
The media thus 'threw a veil' over the glorious and familiar past of the mujahideens. With the Soviets' departure in 1989, the things that these fighters had in common were no longer enough to contain their rivalries. All these warlords' greed and hunger for power relentlessly drove them toward a war of all against all, with alliances broken as soon as they were made. After four years, in 1992 mujahideens took Kabul, over- throwing Najibullah: but the civil war, and above all the war

---

9 Rahim Khushnawaz, *Télérama*, 2714, 16 January 2002, p. 50.
10 Robert Fisk, 'What Will the Northern Alliance Do in Our Name Now?', *Independent*, 14 November 2001.

on civilians, did not stop. The Northern Alliance's soldiers pillaged homes and raped women. Local chiefs ransacked trucks every thirty miles, travel was impossible, and corruption and disorder prevented the application of sharia law.

Some among the mujahideens, in particular the youngest – who took Islamic ideals very seriously indeed – were disheartened. They left to study in Pakistan. These were the *taliban* (students), the spiritual and sometimes biological sons of the mujahideens. They were as anti-communist as their fathers, but more disciplined and serious and even more fundamentalist: in short, they were good candidates for US help, and indeed the latter put up the cash for the Pakistani madrasas (Koranic schools), via Saudi Arabia. In just one year, the formidably armed Taliban conquered a large part of Afghanistan and entered Kabul. When the mujahideens beat a retreat in 1996, they left behind 50,000 dead in Kabul alone, and a city in ruins. Four years of factional warfare produced what six years of struggle against the Soviets had never managed to do.

And what about women?
So did the United States always fight for women's rights? No. Have they ever done so? No. Have they, on the contrary, straightforwardly trampled on women's rights? Yes. After all, women's rights were defended and promoted in Afghanistan from 1978 to 1992, but by Marxist or pro-Soviet governments. That's the period – the era of Amin, Karmak, Taraki and Najibullah – where we find astonishing figures on the number of women doctors, teachers and lawyers. Which is unlucky for the women of Afghanistan: since the government that stood up for them was allied to an enemy of the United States, they had to be sacrificed. We can't let people's rights interfere with the pursuit of world hegemony – particularly if these people are mere women. Women's rights are a bit like Iraqi children: their death is just the price of US power, and the fact that it's

someone else who suffers makes the Americans all the more ready to do without them.

The Taliban's fathers, the mujahideens – this time armed by the Russians who they had chased out twelve years previously – returned to the capital in the shadow of American bombs: and judging by how they waged war, they hadn't changed much.[11] And why would they have changed their approach to women's rights? Why would these men, who took up arms against women's rights before fighting the Soviets and then each other, suddenly have become feminists?

Like all the feminists the world over who spent more than two years on the international campaign protesting the condition of Afghan women under the Taliban, I do hope that the government established in Afghanistan will guarantee women's human rights, and make sure that at least some of these rights are respected in practice. A better status for women could be one unforeseen result of a war: a collateral benefit of some kind. We can hope. But don't count on it.

After all, the Jamiat-e Islami party led by Burnahuddin Rabbani – the president of the legal government recognized by the international community up until the Bonn Agreement [of December 2001] – established sharia law in the Afghan capital in 1992. This is the same party that Massoud belonged to – he was its military commander – and his troops carried out an orgy of rapes and murders when they occupied the Hazara district of Kabul in 1995 during the years of factional strife. Moreover, in February 2002, with the American war still ongoing, the Northern Alliance began to fall apart as the warlords who made up its forces reconquered their lost fiefdoms. Rabbani's largely Tajik party, having arrived in Kabul first, each day extended its control a little further: backed by

---

11 'The Northern Alliance is advancing, meanwhile, with all its baggage of massacres and looting and rape intact', Fisk, 'What Will the Northern Alliance Do in Our Name Now?'

the Russians who now returned to Kabul, Rabbani's party made a power-grab for the majority of the positions in the interim government, in spite of the Americans' wishes. The US did of course succeed in installing Hamid Karzai – a Pashtun – at the head of the interim government, in the place of the Russians' man Rabbani – but he has no real power.[12] Two women – both exiles – are also part of the provisional government: one of them is a member of Hizb-e Wahdat while the other belongs to Parchami. RAWA is strongly critical of both these parties, and indeed of the Northern Alliance's other components.[13]

Pushed by the foreign powers on which all Afghan parties are still dependent, Jamiat-e Islami did make some concessions on the question of women. But let's judge their real content. A spokesman for Rabbani told BBC World one week after the fall of Kabul that 'The Taliban's "restrictions" will be lifted' – without offering any further details – 'and the *burqa* will no longer be compulsory: the *hijab* will suffice'.[14] The *hijab* will suffice: that's the stuff dreams are made of.

---

12 *Human Rights Watch*, 'Military Assistance to the Afghan Opposition', October 2000.

13 Unlike RAWA, Negar – a French-based association 'in support of Afghan women' – backs the Northern Alliance and the bombings. According to this association, Massoud and more recently Karzai signed a 'charter of Afghan women's fundamental rights' (see Christine Delphy's interview of Shoukria Haïdar at cicg.free.fr). This association attributes the horrors of Afghan women's situation to the Taliban alone, never mentioning the mujahideens (*Lesbia*, 208, December 2001, p. 33). One possible explanation of the Negar's siding with the Northern Alliance perhaps resides in the fact that according to Sippi Azerbaijani-Moghadam – technical advisor to the UN commission for refugee women and children, and a specialist on the region – women's organizations have been formed on the basis of the Pashtun, Tajik and Hazara ethnic groups (Sharon Groves, 'Report from Afghanistan', *Feminist Studies*, 27/3, 2001).

14 In its Afghan variant the hijab is the Iranian chador: a cloak enveloping the whole head and body, including the face, and not a simple headscarf.

But had there been more change, would this have justified the war? If standing up for women's rights had been the real reason for the American bombs, would this have justified the attack?

A story (with a moral) and a question: do we have the right to bomb people for their own good?
Once upon a time there was a country where women still didn't have the vote, in spite of thirty years of feminist struggles, years and decades after they had won this right in most neighbouring European countries. How did these other nations treat this country? Did they invade it? Impose sanctions? Withdraw their confidence from it and break off their alliances? On the contrary, they defended it when it was attacked. After victory in 1945 they gave it financial help to rebuild, while asking it to have a bit of a rethink, and give women citizenship. Such it was that in 1945 the women of France got the right to vote.

The right to vote is fundamental. But does that mean I think it's a pity that the US, Britain and the USSR didn't bomb France? No. However valuable this right, if it takes a war to win it then you have to ask whether it is worth the cost. And I regret it all the less because this example shows that there are effective, peaceful means of putting pressure on states.

If we're interested in women's rights – that is, human rights – the question we have to ask about any war is always ultimately the same: what can be worse for a population than war? At what moment does war become the preferable option? To say that the war will help Afghan women means deciding that it's better for them to be killed by bombs, hunger or cold than to live under the Taliban. Better dead than enslaved: such was Western opinion's judgement on the fate of Afghan women. This was hardly a heroic decision, however. What could have made it heroic? Perhaps Rumsfeld, for example, saying, 'I'd rather die than see Afghan women suffer one moment longer under the heel of the Taliban'; that is, the Western powers putting their own necks on the line, rather than those of Afghan women.

What would have been a heroic decision in the first case is, in the second eventuality, just a means of playing with other people's lives, which is morally repugnant. And here we're dealing with this second case. The irresponsible way in which the alibi 'the liberation of Afghan women' is used in the West is an illustration of the fact that Western lives are worth more, infinitely more, than others; as well as the fact that the West, not content with placing a very low price on these other lives, also thinks it has the right to dispose of them at will. Indeed, until recently the decision that the US had made on behalf of Afghan women could only be deduced from a great mass of its leaders' speeches and actions.

The presuppositions of 'the liberation of women' as an alibi; or, the missionary's paradox

But a few days after I had drawn up the first version of this text, this decision and its colonialist assumptions were explicitly posed in an opinion piece in *Le Monde*.[15] 'Can't Franz Xaver Kroetz conceive of Afghan women . . . welcoming the American soldiers (sic)[16] as liberators rather than as kidnappers? The idea that freedom might have a high price, that it might even be worth risking your own life for, seems incomprehensible to at least one peace-lover.' Contrary to

---

15   Peter Schneider, *Le Monde*, 5 December 2001.

16   For Schneider the press's use of the word 'liberation' probably evoked the image of French women embracing American soldiers during the liberation of Paris. But this was not France in 1944. In the Afghanistan of 2001, the American soldiers were nowhere to be seen: rather, it was the Northern Alliance troops, whose reputation was not exactly that of 'liberators', who entered Kabul.

appearances, the life of which this author speaks is not *his* life. At the very moment that he says that Afghan women's freedom is worth sacrificing their lives for, he denies them their freedom: after all, he is making this 'choice' for them. This contradiction is not specific to him alone: rather, it pervades the whole Western attitude toward Afghan women; it is more generally the organizing principle behind the attitude of the dominant toward the dominated.

I would like to suggest a simple rule of international moral conduct that could also apply to relations among individuals: we have no right to make decisions, above all heroic ones, when people other than us have to bear the consequences. The only population who can decide whether a war is worth the cost are the people who will have to pay this price. In this case, by contrast, the people who have decided in favor of the war do not have to undergo it; whereas the people on the sharp end have no say in the matter. And so far, the humanitarian war hasn't lived up to its promises. Millions of Afghan women are in the streets, in tents and in camps. Before the war, 4.5 million Afghans lived in refugee camps in Pakistan and Iran, and since then even more have come to join them, fleeing the American bombs. We don't know their exact numbers, since many of these people are hiding for fear of being forced to go back: nonetheless, estimates suggest that Pakistan and Iran have taken in 700,000 and 300,000 more people respectively.

But the people most in danger – and the hardest to count – are the 'internally displaced' who simply try to escape the bombs, and who have had to keep moving along with the front line. They are today living in improvized camps, without food or protection against the men roving around with guns. To this day no international aid has reached these people, on account of the territory being divided up into fiefdoms controlled by the poorly supplied troops of the warlords – 'soldiers by day, bandits by night'. When aid organizations do persist in trying to bring them help, these armed gangs hijack it.

Many refugees have died or will soon die,[17] especially among the 'internally displaced' and the populations of the mountain plateaus, who have been deprived of food aid since September on account of the war, and who are now isolated by snow. As in all wars and all famines, this death toll will include a disproportionately high number of women: and without any guarantee that this 'sacrifice' will earn them any more rights.

But this is a temporary situation, some will say: once peace has returned, the food supplies will resume and the country will be rebuilt. We are still far from that, then; the reconstruction of Afghanistan requires peace, and peace is exactly what the Afghans don't have.

The United States has made use of the warlords who sowed ruin in Afghanistan before 1996: 700,000 armed men roving around a country that is now more ravaged than ever before. Ethnic divisions, already aggravated during the first civil war of 1992–96, deteriorated still further thanks to the Taliban, which was contemptuous of all non-Pashtuns. With their defeat, the classic rivalry among warlords was compounded by the desire of the Hazaras, Tajiks and Uzbeks for revenge on the Pashtuns. On 10 January, RAWA demanded the urgent intervention of an international force to 'protect the Afghan people against the Northern Alliance criminals'.[18] A few days later, Karzai begun denouncing the reprisals against the Pashtuns in the regions where they are in the minority: he then took advantage of a visit to New York to demand that the UN

---

17   There is no tally of these deaths (or of the direct victims of US bombings) but in December 2001 some American humanitarian organizations put the figure at 3,700.

18   'The "Northern Alliance": The Most Murderous Violations of Human Rights!', 10 December 2001, www.rawa.org.

send an international police force, having previously only asked for money.[19] The resumption of the civil war, whose early signs were already visible during the fight against the Taliban, for example in the capture of Kunduz, is now more and more openly declared. The Pashtun governor of Kandahar, Gul Agha Sherzai, has sent 20,000 men to dispute control of Herat with the Tajik Ismail Khan.[20] Fighting has broken out in the North in the Kunduz region, and in the South East around Khost. There have been clashes in Mazar-i-Sharif setting the Uzbek Abdul Rashid Dostum's forces against those of the Tajik Atta Mohammed, while in Gardez, in the South East, the governor appointed by Karzai, Pacha Khan Zadran, battled with the local elder Haji Saifullah, at the cost of sixty lives.[21] Even the best-protected city, Kabul, has fallen victim to this disorder. A diplomat posted in the capital remarked that its residents no longer go to certain parts of the city: 'Kalashnikov culture rules here.'[22]

But the United States is otherwise occupied flattening the Tora Bora mountains, and it has repeatedly reiterated its lack of appetite for 'nation building': it destroys but doesn't repair the damage. So there will be no international force to protect the country as a whole: it will comprise just 4,500 men, posted in Kabul and its surroundings, and for just six months.[23] The United States does not want to tie up the soldiers it would take to control the 700,000 armed men roving around Afghan territory, and nor will it allow other countries – necessarily including Russia – to do so. The Taliban, now transformed back into ordinary citizens (as one Afghan showed a Western reporter, all it takes is wrapping their turbans a bit differently)

19   BBC World, 30 January 2002.
20   *Globe and Mail*, 22 January 2002.
21   AP and *Time Magazine Newsletter*, 1–7 February 2002.
22   *Hindustan Times*, quoted by AFP, 25 January 2002.
23   *Hindustan Times*, 20 January 2002.

want to resume service under the Pashtun lords. They will bring them their taste for war – they know nothing else – and their hatred of the Tajiks and Uzbeks.

The West has not brought peace and prosperity: it has destroyed what was left to be destroyed, made even more people flee a country that had already been bled dry, cut off the food supply to a population dying of hunger, and given arms back to warlords who dream of nothing but privileges, conquests and massacres. Before the war we thought it impossible that Afghanistan could fall into an even more dire state than it was in already: but it really could get worse, and we've made it so.

Today's 'duty to intervene', yesterday's 'civilizing mission'
If they had the least decency the Allies would stop claiming that they're imposing all this on Afghan women (and men) for their own good; and above all, they would stop pretending that they are taking away Afghans' right to choose their own fate – and even their right to life – in the name of their freedom. But we have good reason to worry that this couplet might become something of a hit. After all, there is a long list of countries that the coalition of Allies-against-evil have promised to save by military means.[24] And of course, any resemblance to past historic events – so long in the past that even their names are old hat – and any resemblance to colonial wars is just a coincidence.

---

24   On 31 January, Bush reiterated for the fifth time since 9/11 that the United States wants to wage war on a global scale, introducing yet more countries into the mix. He targeted Iran and North Korea, and also Hamas, Hezbollah and Islamic Jihad. Two days later, the first American troops arrived in the Philippines. For three months Western media and public opinion have dismissed these statements as so much bluster. Without doubt, it will take the bombing of another country – likely in the not-too-distant future – for these statements to be taken for what they really are: a programme, and not just comments made for rhetorical effect.

War will never advance human rights. Even apart from what's been done to the Afghans, this war in the name of civilization has in two months thrown a good part of this civilization itself into the dustbin of history. For starters, the Geneva Conventions. These have been declared invalid by the Allies, complicit first in the crimes of the butcher of Mazar-i-Sharif ('General' Dostum, deputy defence minister in the Karzai government) and others;[25] and now complicit in the American manoeuvres inventing new pseudo-legal categories, like the 'unlawful combatants' held at Guantánamo, who are not covered by any national or international law, nor by any of the laws of war or by any common law![26] Civil liberties – the pride of our democracies – have been trampled upon. Meanwhile, international law has suffered a fatal blow: the lumbering corpse of the UN, now in its death agony, is there to prove it.

Only a genuine, peaceful cooperation among nations would advance human rights. But that's not on the table today. Not only are the war's real goals entirely different from the arguments used to 'sell' it to public opinion, but these 'humanitarian' or 'humanist' arguments are themselves fundamentally flawed. The reasoning of the opinion piece mentioned above, for example, is based on the same arguments that the Spanish monks typically used with regard to the Indians in the New World. This postulate tells us that we (the West) know what's best for everyone, and have the right – or perhaps the duty – to propose it to or impose it on the rest of the world. These others, who are intellectually and morally inferior to us, don't have the same value that we do: and in consequence, their lives are worth less than ours.

---

25 Robert Fisk: 'We are the War Criminals Now', *Independent*, 29 November 2001; Human Rights Watch, www.hrw.org, 1 December 2001; cicg.free.fr, 29 November 2001.

26 See www.hrw.org, 22 January 2002; cicg.free.fr, 23 January 2002; www.amnesty.org, letter to Mr. Bush, 21 January 2002.

The civilian populations of the coalition countries have no direct interest in imperialist wars. Their rulers' real motives do not 'motivate' them: the legitimacy of these wars is diminished in the people's eyes when economic arguments are brought into the frame. Governments always paint their wars in disinterested or even noble colours: if not as the only justification, at least as an auxiliary argument or something to help swallow the pill. The Gulf War was indeed seen by public opinion as a war 'for oil' but also as a 'just war' – one reason provided a pass for another. The Serbia war – the most popular war – is credited with having prevented genocide. It is possible that there is some duplicity in public opinion, and that it really does agree with the self-interested reasons for going to war. But it certainly doesn't emphasize this: the people prefer to leave the cynicism to the politicians.

In the case of the Afghan war, French public opinion accepted a hotchpotch of reasons; some of them of little moral weight, such as the desire for revenge. But this shameful motive had to be 'balanced out' by something else; it would be unseemly for the war's only goal to be to martyrize yet further one of the poorest and most hard-done-by populations on the planet; the war had to bear the promise of something good, or at least less bad, for the Afghan people, such that they could receive some sort of 'recompense' for their suffering.

That is why the issue of Afghan women was crucial, even though it was raised rather belatedly: because it provided the necessary 'altruistic' and 'moral' dimension to the conflict. But as we have seen, this motif was in fact a mask for denying free choice and even life itself to the people it targeted. So what kind of ethical framework does this moral cause belong to: and to what extent is it really 'altruistic'?

The moral justification – in this case, 'the liberation of Afghan women' – appealed to what look like progressive values. But they are only apparently progressive, because on closer inspection they amount to the more or less conscious belief in the West's 'mission'; and we believe in such a mission because we believe that we are 'civilized'. Since the 9/11 attacks, no journalist, no politician, and no intellectual has criticized the equation that Bush and his epigones draw between the West and civilization – on the contrary, there is total consensus that terrorism represents 'an attack against civilization'. The actions of the Western powers in the non-Western world are supported by a public whose worldview has not fundamentally changed since the end of colonization. The belief in the West's superiority remains intact. This racism – and it is racism, however explicit or implicit – is today allied with a paternalistic compassion: and combining the two produces an ideology that is potentially very dangerous to non-Westerners and to dominated peoples and groups more generally. After all, today it is used as justification for military intervention as well as humanitarian action, and sometimes both at once – as we saw when the American public approved of the simultaneous dropping of bombs and aid parcels. Feeding them and punishing them: that's the responsibility of parents toward their children, no? George W. Bush's vocabulary is very revealing in this regard: whether he's talking to his allies or his enemies, he speaks the language of a firm but fair father who dishes out encouragement and disapproval, reward and punishment according to his kids' behaviour. Equally telling is the fact that Western public opinion seems not to be taken aback by this condescension, which suggests that people do identify with Bush's position.

Without here making any attempt to link these attitudes to Western governments' real actions over the last fifty years, what we can see is that the ideological changes heralded by decolonization, the UN charter, the recognition of people's right to self-determination and all the other international conventions do not seem to be reflected in today's common sense, or to have been able to influence it. The words have changed, but it is not difficult to see the shadow of the 'civilizing mission' of yesteryear in the new talk of 'the duty to intervene'. And it is still just as murderous, incorporating the missionary's paradox: 'We will save their souls (their freedom) even if we have to kill them to do so.'

CHAPTER 7

Against an Exclusionary Law

It is generally believed that the only real target of the law banning the wearing of religious symbols is the 'veil', also known as the Islamic headscarf.

This law will make it easier to expel girls who wear the headscarf from school. It is a bill that divides all political groups and all civil society associations, and also divides feminists. The partisans of this bill are in the majority within each of these groups. Difficult discussions have shown that rational arguments do not play much of a role in determining their belief. They can't bear to see the headscarf, and they don't even want to talk with the girls who wear the 'veil'. As one member of the Stasi commission put it, they didn't think it worth holding hearings with those concerned, since they were not 'predisposed to their arguments' . . . so much so that they didn't even want to hear them.[1] Unfortunately most of our fellow citizens are of this same disposition, summed up by the feminist who explained that the veil is a 'symbol of oppression'. And that's it. The implicit conclusion – which explains the refusal to hear out the women concerned – is that only alienated, manipulated people could wear a symbol of oppression. And what would be the point of discussion with the alienated and the manipulated? So immediately the dividing lines are drawn: we know what the thing you're wearing means,

---

1 Named after its chair, Bernard Stasi, this commission on French secularism [*laïcité*] was set up on the orders of President Jacques Chirac in 2003 – *translator's note*.

we known better than you what you're doing, and nothing that you could say will undermine our certainties, backed up by our main certainty: that we are right, that we own truth and knowledge. When we decide that part of the population is not in control of its behaviour or its senses – the very definition of mental illness – then discussion is not only futile, but even dangerous. After all, it would mean them getting within touching distance of us; they might even contaminate us with their pathological discourse.

The only thing that we can do for these people is to try and protect them from themselves and from those who manipulate them; and if that's too difficult, then at least we can stop them contaminating others, by putting them out of sight – sorry, I mean, out of the classrooms.

So we'll trash these girls' fundamental right to education, under the pretext that their presence could *potentially* threaten others' right not to wear the headscarf. As well as considering these young women alienated, we're imputing to them some rather malign intentions: it seems that their plan is to make it compulsory to wear the veil in France! Who could have imagined six months ago that these two thousand girls, most of whom are from a so-called 'immigrant background' (that extremely strange birthplace that doesn't appear on any map of France), wield such great power over the country?

It is only in adopting such a paranoid perspective that we can understand why the exclusion of these girls has become the top political priority. Only starting from this delirium can we understand the perverse reasoning that justifies destroying one freedom in the name of *defending another*, even if this latter is not being attacked at the moment and is, to tell the truth, un-attackable. It's the same reasoning that lies behind the launching of so-called 'pre-emptive' wars – so much in fashion today – attacking in the name of preventing an imaginary danger. Here, too, the danger is an imaginary one: not only does no one have any intention of making it compulsory to wear the veil in France, but most importantly no one would even be able to do so. Meanwhile, once the war is under way, its destructive dynamic – tearing apart societies as well as human lives – continues apace.

In the war launched in France in the name of heading off the 'Islamist danger' – whose existence *in this country* no one can prove – the dynamic of conflict will gather momentum and become ever more aggravated, just like we see in other pre-emptive wars. Even if the danger is a fantasy – as we see when we subject it to any scrutiny – the war itself will be a real one, and it will have its victims: in the first place the young women excluded by a state reneging on its obligation to school all children. The second victim, meanwhile, will be the possibility of reconciliation between the community of North African origin, which rightly feels wounded by decades of discrimination, and the rest of the country.

So how do sociologists – whether feminist or otherwise – analyse the adoption of the Muslim faith, and, in these girls' case, the wearing of the headscarf? As a reaction to the fact of having been excluded from the national community both symbolically and materially, and still being excluded from it even today. Even the political class (Left and Right both), even the bill's partisans, and even the members of the Stasi commission recognize that this is all playing out against a backdrop of ghettoization and discrimination at all levels of society, particularly in the labour market. But we don't want to see discrimination; no, France isn't racist, only Le Pen is a racist: but then how come the descendants of North African immigrants are four times more likely to fall victim to unemployment than other people with the same qualifications?

Some do recognize this problem, but find the reaction of the people concerned rather unseemly: 'Your grievances are real', they say, 'but your response is mistaken.' As a feminist I

know that the revolt of the dominated rarely takes the form
that would best please the dominant. I could even say: it never
takes the form that suits them. Let's go further: what the dominant want is for us to ask politely for our rights, and even if
after forty years of waiting we don't get what we wanted, we
ought to act like it doesn't matter. And it is indeed true that
it's no problem for men if male violence against women is
eradicated tomorrow or in a hundred years' time. And it's no
problem for whites if racism is eradicated tomorrow or in a
hundred years' time.

Conversely, the dominant do see a serious problem in the
oppressed 'reacting the wrong way'. That's what we urgently
need to correct, repress and stamp out. The political class tells
us – with a touching spirit of unity – that they have identified
the cause of the problem, but first they're going to attack its
consequence – your unseemly reaction – and they'll leave
addressing its causes for another day . . . that is, never. We,
Féministes pour l'égalité, say: if we have to start by addressing
any one thing, we should begin by turning to where the
problem starts, as foreign as that logic might be to our political
class.

The illness from which France suffers is not the fact that
two thousand girls wear the headscarf – for various reasons,
which are their own reasons and which they are free to have,
since they have not committed any crime. And what are their
crimes meant to be? Where are the women they've beaten to
death, or the children that they have raped? The illnesses from
which this country suffers are, firstly, a patent, brutal, institutional, omnipresent, systemic sexism, and a patent, brutal,
institutional, omnipresent, systemic racism, which govern the
policies of the employers, the housing offices, the ANPE
[state-run employment bureau] and Le Pen. The political class
has chosen to turn its gaze away from this serious illness, so
that it can focus exclusively on its symptoms. Directly tackling

a culture in which racist and sexist discrimination is banalized to the point of becoming the norm and not the exception – well, that would take some effort. A lot of work, that. Meanwhile, reasserting their principles and stigmatizing an already oppressed minority doesn't take any trouble – or so they believe, blind to the long-term consequences of their demagogy.

The consequences of this collective blindness and the law springing from it are, indeed, worrying. All this can only exacerbate the justified resentment felt by the descendants of North African immigrants, suspected of belonging to some sort of fifth column just because they seek a dignity they haven't found in a republican equality that's gone AWOL. For this reason, the law opens the way to all sorts of extremists, including Muslim extremists – for why would there be no extremists among their number, when there's extremists everywhere else?

Let's try to see the positive side: a link has now been established between feminists and the girls who wear the veil, many of whom have developed a feminism that goes with their Islam and not against it. And why not? We have long been in dialogue with women who are both Catholic and feminist, Protestant and feminist, or Jewish and feminist. And if I finish with this pink light in a leaden sky, it is because yesterday in a meeting of 'progressives' I saw and heard the most shameful colonial and racist arrogance being expressed, and was greatly disheartened by this. If this evening I try to convince you that some good can come out of the bad, it's firstly because I'm trying to convince myself of that; and I'm hoping that you'll help me.

CHAPTER 8

Race, Caste and Gender in France

The subject of this text is the situation of the descendants of ex-colonized North African immigrants in contemporary France – a condition that everyone admits is 'problematic'. My hypothesis, which I already put forward in 2001, is that today in France we are witnessing the creation of a system of racial castes. Sociologists and political scientists in France do not use the concept of 'castes', whether they are Marxists or otherwise.[1] However, in my view this concept is of some use for explaining the specific place of racial oppression within the class system: for which the concept of racism is insufficient. Indeed, while the concept of racism lays emphasis on process, 'caste' instead stresses the results of this process, in terms of the social structure. It struck me that the situation of the descendants of these immigrants has not followed the same processes as other immigrant groups' descendants, and that they have 'inherited' their parents' social inferiority.

I will try to demonstrate this social 'immobility' of the so-called 'Maghrebian' [North African] group, and identify some of its mechanisms, including the aggravation of the racism against them. I will also examine the way in which the social construct 'race' is articulated with that other social construct known as 'sex'. These social constructs are built in the same way, through domination and for the purposes of domination, though they obviously take distinct forms. The debate

---

1 Christine Delphy, 'La transmission héréditaire', in *L'Ennemi principal*, Vol. I.

on the Islamic headscarf does play some role in this interaction and interlinking of sexism and racism, but mostly as a telling moment of crisis.

Indeed, this situation is not a static one, and the crisis over the headscarf is typical of the dynamic of oppression in general, and thus also of 'racial' oppression. We can see it as a repressive response to a rebellion. But this rebellion itself followed a period of oppression. This sequence – oppression, rebellion, repression – explains the dynamic behind the treatment of 'immigrants and their descendants'. I also see this sequence as a French tragedy, since the rebellion should have led to liberation, and not the increased oppression that resulted from its repression.

In each of these phases, the thing that interests me is the way in which gender – a caste system based on the invention of different sexes – is used to construct a caste system based on the invention of different races.

Act I: oppression
The first act, oppression, dates back to conquest and the colonization of Algeria, now more than a hundred and fifty years ago, and then that of the other countries of North Africa a century ago. Unlike what happened in Indochina, religion was the basis of the differential treatment expressed in the '*indigénat*' status imposed on the colonized peoples. In 1945 the status of *indigénat* was dismantled. In theory all men (for women it came only years later) were citizens. But after negotiations with white settlers, the population of Algeria was divided into two categories of citizens: 'French men of European stock' (whites) and 'Muslim Frenchmen', voting in different 'colleges'. The end result was that the vote of one Frenchman of European stock was worth the vote of five Muslim Frenchmen.

Since the beginning of colonization, the question of sex, or gender, set the dividing line between the two 'communities' that were thus created. According to the colonial power's racist stereotype, the indigenous North African men 'treated women badly'. Polygamy in particular was considered a sign or even *the* sign of indigenous men's 'backwardness', even though it was in fact an uncommon practice.[2]

'Muslim French' status had the effect of subjecting the women of this community to a civil code for marriage, parentage and inheritance called 'personal status', which was considered to be 'trailing behind' the French code. Nonetheless, we should emphasize here that apart from the question of polygamy the French civil code of that era – between 1830 and 1962 – was hardly any less detrimental to women than the Muslim French one was, especially before the Second World War. Allowing mass exemption from the civil code in one French *département* certainly did have deleterious effects on indigenous women, who like women of French stock were not considered citizens until the end of the Second World War. But it also allowed for a continued denigration of Islam. In truth, this was nothing new: maligning Islam has a long tradition in Europe, stretching back to the age of the Spanish *Reconquista* and the Crusades.[3]

Thus gender – which establishes a hierarchical division splitting the human species into two opposed categories, men and women – served as the dividing line for a further separation, between two 'ethnicities'. And these, too, were fabricated by domination – in this case, colonial domination.

In occupied Algeria, 'natives' of male sex could escape their status as sub-citizens, but only on condition that they

---

2   Julia Clancy-Smith, 'La femme arabe: Women and Sexuality in France's North African Empire', *Women, the Family and Divorce Laws in Islamic History*, Syracuse: Syracuse University Press, 1996.

3   Norman Daniel, *Islam et Occident,* Paris: Éditions du Cerf, 1993; Vincent Geisser, *La Nouvelle Islamophobie*, Paris: La Découverte, 2003.

renounced their religion, culture, beliefs, family and neighbours. As such, on the ideological and legal plane, Islam became the reason that was given for their inferior status as *indigènes*. This allowed for the principal, objective reason – occupation and colonization – to be obscured.

Following the conquest of Algeria, the denigration of Islam became centered on the classically colonial opposition between the 'civilized' and the 'barbaric'. And no less classically, this counterposition also concerned the relations between the sexes. When the colonizers spoke of indigenous women – ignoring their own patriarchy, which they doubtless considered normal, just like today – it was always with tears in their eyes. They only referred to the differences between these two patriarchal regimes – the French one and the Algerian one – at the cost of any mention of their far more considerable commonalities.

Indeed, one central point is systematically passed over in silence in studies on colonization and in today's studies on racism or discrimination. Namely, that *the relations between the colonizing society and the colonized society are also the relations between two patriarchies.* The protagonists of the colonial conflict on both sides were men. In each of the two societies, only men had the status of subjects; women were objects, property. It is logical enough that the colonizer wanted to dispossess the indigenous men of their most precious possession, indeed the last one that was left to them: women. A nineteenth-century French official cited by Frantz Fanon said, 'If we are to strike against Algerian society's capacity to resist, then we must first of all conquer their women', adding, 'We have to go and find these women, under the veils they hide behind.'

In fact, the French did nothing to help North African women. But they did carry out a few 'un-veiling' campaigns during the Algerian war, already back then under the pretext

of 'liberating women'. In reality, the purpose of these campaigns – like the rapes committed by soldiers or the use of
'lascivious' native women in brothels – was to demoralize the
Algerian men by 'stealing' their last bit of property: women.
And since the colonizer blared the trumpets of women's liberation in the interest of destroying the autochthonous identity,
those fighting for independence logically enough rejected it,
presenting the maintenance and strengthening of the hierarchy
between the sexes as a constituent part of their national
project.[4]

Let's jump forward a few decades. Now the North African
countries are independent. The former colonial subjects were
already present in the metropolis before independence, and
they came in even greater numbers afterwards.

Three historical events created a problem for the so-called
'people of European stock' – which means whites – and there
is one that they have still not managed to resolve. This immigration was long purely masculine, comprising men only. But
the immigrants who wanted to go back often found that they
couldn't; then, in 1974, the law on family reunion allowed
them to bring their wives to France. Finally, the French nationality law, despite the changes made to it, kept the element of
jus soli, and their children became French. French society had
not foreseen this series of events. It did not see that the combination of family reunion and *jus soli* would place it in a
situation where the children of former colonial subjects theoretically have exactly the same rights as any other French
citizen.

French society only offers them the same status as their
parents had, while these children of the Republic, sure of their
rights, demand their due as French citizens – and they insist

---

4   Monique Gadant, *Le Nationalisme algérien et les femmes*, Paris:
l'Harmattan, 1995.

on this ever more noisily and ever more 'arrogantly', as the minister Xavier Darcos put it. This is what Farad Khosrokhavar[5] called the 'misunderstanding' between French society and the descendants of immigrants; I would call it France's dilemma. France does not want to accept them, but nor can it send them 'back home', because they have no home other than France. Having to find a third way – obstinately refusing to accept them, but unable to kick them out – it has tried to uphold and strengthen a caste system. And one of the ways of doing so is to criminalize Islam.

After the war, immigrants were treated more or less as they had been when they were colonized. But as guest workers they made few demands (though an 'Arab Workers' Movement' existed between 1945 and the beginning of the Algerian war). They accepted the hardest jobs, the lowest salaries and being penned into the *bidonville* slums. Their only goal was to be able to send money back home and build a house there. Keeping their heads down and putting up with racism was just the price they had to pay for the eventual recompense of being able to return to Algeria. This light at the end of the tunnel kept them going, even if they didn't all get there. This explains their patience, their humility and their resignation to practising their religion in cellars rather than mosques. Today French people are nostalgic for this Islam – of which they were ignorant when it did exist – honouring it with the label 'traditional', as if it were a Camembert AOC.[6] Except that here 'traditional' doesn't mean ladle-moulded, but invisible. The best Islam, in a way: in any case the only suitable one, i.e. the only one that suits us.

---

5   Farad Khosrokhavar, *L'Islam des jeunes,* Paris: Flammarion, 1997.

6   EU certification of products (wines, cheeses, etc.) made in the regions with which they are traditionally associated and according to 'authentic' methods – *translator's note.*

But the hope of recompense that allowed the immigrant parents to put up with this situation does not exist for their descendants. Yet it seems that the immigrant status of the parents of Maghrebians and Africans has been passed down across the generations, both materially and in terms of other people's perceptions. That is, they still imagine that these people are destined one day to leave French territory. *And when people inherit exactly the same status that their parents had, with no probability or even possibility of social mobility, then what we're dealing with is a caste situation, not a class situation.* That's what's now being created in France. We even see it in language: when we speak of 'second-' or even 'third-generation immigrants', we transform the immigrant condition – which is, by definition, temporary – into a hereditary and almost biological trait.

This racism has long been made light of, understood as a matter of certain people's overtly racist attitudes and not in terms of the objective treatment of the population concerned.[7] But we do know that this population suffers enormous discrimination, whether in housing, education, or employment or in terms of judicial repression.[8]

Hardly ever studied, however, is the mental suffering that racism induces in its victims. This was very clear during the debate 'on the veil'. Discrimination was only mentioned as an afterthought to the discussion, in the euphemized form of references to 'failed integration'. Moreover, such 'failures' were

---

7   Patrick Simon, 'La statistique des origines: l'ethnicité et la "race" dans les recensements aux États-Unis, Canada et Grande-Bretagne', *Sociétés contemporaines*, 26, 1997, pp. 11–44; Maryse Tripier, 'De l'enjeu des statistiques "ethniques"', *Hommes et migrations*, 1219, 1999, pp. 27–31.

8   S. Beaud and M. Pialoux, *Violences urbaines, violences sociales*, Paris: Fayard, 2003; Michèle Tribalat, *Faire France. Une enquête sur les immigrés et leurs enfants*, Paris: La Découverte, 1995.

attributed to the discriminated-against population itself, alleg-edly having chosen to live 'among themselves' twenty miles from the city centre and refusing to mix in with 'people of French stock', seemingly out of snobbery. This common-sense point of view was also the official stance of the Interior Ministry.[9]

As for those concerned, they know well enough that society excludes them. In the 1980s they organized an imposing 'march for equality' across the whole country. But the movement was recuperated by the Parti Socialiste, which created SOS-Racisme for the purposes of neutralizing these protests . . . and suc-ceeded in doing so. This respectful, 'properly French' revolt – with its secular, republican protests – failed lamentably.[10]

Act II: rebellion

Thus the bitterness caused by this failure compounded this population's bitter everyday experience of racism. They played the game, and it didn't work.

As for the Franco-French, they are no longer concerned with discrimination or ghettos. Rather, they're preoccupied by the integration or non-integration of youths of North African origin. But the meaning they attribute to the word 'integration' is biased: in TV reports and political statements, this always refers to how much effort the children of Maghrebians are making to fully resemble the children of Bretons or Auvergnats. Sometimes they manage without too much trouble; at other times, they have to renounce their own identity. For example, talking about your childhood is an important part of sociability. In the case of Bretons and Auvergnats it is allowed or even

9 Sylvie Tissot, 'Le "repli communautaire": un concept policier. Analyse d'un rapport des Renseignements généraux sur les "quartiers sen-sibles" ', http://lmsi.net/spip.php?article3 22&var_recherche=tissot.

10 Saïd Bouamama, *Dix ans de marche des Beurs, Chronique d'un mouvement avorté*, Paris: Desclée de Brouwer, 1994.

encouraged, with people from rural areas and city-dwellers marvelling at the similarities and differences between their respective experiences. But no one's interested in your Arab parents: you'd best not mention them. This population is thus caught in a formidable double bind: they are called on to show that they're 'the same' but they are perceived and labelled as 'different'. Whatever they do, in the end they always fail the exam, and they will never manage to satisfy the criteria of Frenchness. The unspoken reality is that these criteria exclude anyone of Maghrebian or African origin *by definition*.

Several generations obeyed these contradictory racist and sexist injunctions, which exhort the dominated to erase and yet simultaneously be comfortable with their 'difference'. But that changed when some of them understood that this whole game deliberately sets out to exhaust them physically and mentally; that the 'difference' they're labelled with is nothing other than an inferior status; and that they cannot be at ease with this difference unless they accept their own inferiority, which they can't shake off because – according to racism's essentialist thinking – it is indelibly inscribed on their bodies. Ultimately, they discover that there is a hidden clause: inclusion has a racial condition that they could never satisfy, because they aren't of the right race.

What can the people and groups caught in this kind of double bind do about it? What do you do when you are attacked for your appearance, your parents, and your origins: all the things for which you aren't responsible and cannot change? Well, you can either live in shame, or else revolt against this injustice. You can either kneel down and accept defeat, or else turn around and face your aggressors. Facing up to them means asserting what you are attacked for, refusing to be ashamed. And this is what French society terms 'communitarian' reactions, which supposedly deserve condemnation. Why? Because when the dominant assigned these identities to the dominated, they did so in order to make them accept their inferior status; and not so that the dominated could make use of these identities in order to rebuild their self-esteem destroyed by racism or sexism.

For a decade now the descendants of immigrants have been rejecting the idea that their origins are a source of shame; they assert an 'Arabness' and an Islam 'made in France', created as a response to exclusion. Some might call this 'identitarian', or a mark of pride, or anti-racism; but certainly it does not stand in contradiction with their rights and demands as citizens. If the dominant society sees this self-assertion as subversive, that's because it's a means by which the dominated resist internalizing an inferior status, and repair what Goffman called a 'damaged identity'.[11] But the dominant society *wants* the dominated to hold onto a damaged identity; this being one of the conditions of perpetuating their exploitation.

The Franco-French thought that the descendants of immigrants would simply accept stepping into their parents' shoes: they were shocked when the children of immigrants took seriously the paperwork telling them they were French.

What is the role of gender in this caste system? After all, the hostility of this discourse is mainly directed against those perceived as the only subjects: men. Women are exempt from the worst stereotypes. The *beurettes* [female, 'second generation immigrants'] are pleasant enough,[12] unlike their brothers, the bad boys (or Arab boys – it's the same difference, as Nacira Guénif-Souilamas tells us).[13] That explains why they face an even more difficult dilemma than men do. Subjected to the double bind of integration, a test they cannot pass, women are

---

11   Erving Goffmann, *Stigma: Notes on the Management of Spoiled Identity*, Englewood Cliffs, NJ: Prentice-Hall, 1964.

12   Nacira Guénif-Souilamas, *Des beurettes*, Paris: Grasset, 2000.

13   Nacira Guénif-Souilamas and Eric Macé, *Les Féministes et le garçon arabe*, Paris: L'Aube, 2004.

also the target of a subliminal injunction. Indeed, these kindly *beurettes* are more pitied than blamed – that is, pitied for belonging to these men, these Arab fathers and Arab boys. And they're told to abandon them. Some obey, leaving their families and neighbourhoods, only to find themselves isolated. After all, here, too, Franco-French society imposes the same double bind we saw earlier: it seeks and finds in these women the difference – in their names, their facial features or their accents – that marks them as essential inferiority, their 'human stain'. So as Christelle Hamel explains,[14] these women are caught between the very real sexism of their own surroundings – a sexism exacerbated by counter-racism, that is, men taking pride in the machismo that they're reproached for – and the dominant society's desire to capture them from the men it still sees as its enemies. This was the context for the 'headscarf controversies' of 1989, 1994[15] and 2003, this latter case ultimately culminating in the 'anti-veil law'.[16] We cannot understand these controversies, nor the reasons underlying the persecution of schoolchildren who posed no problem to their teachers, unless we understand the prominent role of gender in this caste system.

We've seen that colonial ideology characterizes Maghrebian, Arab and African men in terms of their relation to women; and the colonial strategy consists of condemning this culture as particularly sexist. At the same time, following a fine patriarchal logic, it tries to capture the women from these same backgrounds, symbolically, at least.

---

14 Christelle Hamel, 'L'intrication des rapports sociaux de sexe, de "race", d'âge et de classe: ses effets sur la gestion des risques d'infection par le VIH chez les Français descendant de migrants du Maghreb', Paris: Thèses, EHESS, 2003.

15 Françoise Gaspard and Farad Khosrokhavar, *Le Foulard et la République*, Paris: La Découverte, 1995.

16 Saïd Bouamama, *L'Affaire du foulard islamique, la production d'un racisme respectable*, Paris: Le Geai bleu, 2004.

A good measure of this unspoken desire is the national joy whenever *beurettes* denounce Arab men, for example when gang rapes come to light.[17] Collective rapes, which have always existed, have never captured public attention and we never hear them mentioned, any more than discussion of rape in general.[18] But when this is going on among the North Africans in the *banlieues*, all France pretends to have discovered a phenomenon that was hitherto unknown in the Hexagon.[19] And it exploits the differentness imposed on Arabs in order to crush in the womb any attempt to recognize and combat its own, purely autochthonous sexist barbarism. It uses circular reasoning to arrive at this conclusion: if they, who are different from us, are getting up to all this, then that's evidence enough that it isn't happening among our own kind. This sophism allows France to kill two birds with one stone: not only can it use it to condemn the 'others', but above all it can absolve itself of the sin now being 'exposed'.[20]

Here I ought to speak of what I think are the reasons why the sight of a few headscarves has plunged France into what Emmanuel Terray has called 'political hysteria'.[21]

The colonized deserved to be colonized because they were uncivilized and had a barbarous culture based on a barbarous religion; and their treatment of their women was proof of this barbarism. The colonized women, the victims of their men – unlike civilized men, who only kill six of their women a month

17   See p. 155
18   Christelle Hamel, '"Faire tourner les meufs": les viols collectifs dans les discours des médias et des agresseurs', *Gradiva* 33, 2003, pp. 85–92.
19   *L'Hexagone* = metropolitan France, as distinct from the French Republic including its various non-European *départements* and territories – *translator's note*.
20   Christine Delphy, 'Une affaire française', in C. Nordmann, *Le Foulard islamique en question*, Paris: Amsterdam, 2004.
21   Emmanuel Terray, 'Une hystérie politique', in C. Nordmann, *Le Foulard islamique en question*.

(at least) – were thus the colonizers' natural allies, if only they would rally to the cause. If they did, then the colonized men would be deprived of their greatest support, and it would also prove how barbaric their treatment of women was. This hope still exists among the French, who treat immigrants like colonial subjects and the children of the colonized as immigrants. In reality, the women are racialized just as much as the men: discriminated against and humiliated every day.

When women wearing the headscarf appeared, the French were shocked – politicians, journalists and secular activists repeated *ad infinitum* – because they are so attached to equality between men and women. One reader of the LDH [Human Rights League] bulletin even wrote that 'the headscarf tears a hole in equality between the sexes'. It was here that I first learned that women in France are men's equals. But enough pleasantries. I don't believe that the French are shocked by the absence of something that doesn't exist, and which they don't really want to exist. Yes, they were 'assaulted', as Chirac put it: the appearance of these women in headscarves upset their unspoken, irrational hopes.

Effectively, they refused to live with the descendants of Arabs, but also couldn't just drive them into the sea. My hypothesis is that faced with this unanswerable dilemma they hatched a plan: if they took these women, even taking them as their wives – as Emmanuel Todd predicted a decade ago[22] – then given that women are nothing more than receptacles for men's semen, this 'race' would soon disappear. This plan – which in France is unconscious rather than explicit – has been the basis of government policies enacted in other racist countries. For example, in the 1950s Brazil had an explicit policy of encouraging mixed marriages in order to 'whiten' the population.

---

22   Emmanuel Todd, *Le Destin des immigrés*, Paris: Seuil, 1997.

But the headscarf told the Franco-French that their dream of dividing the descendants of immigrants along gender lines was finished. These women would not reject their fathers, brothers and husbands. They did not believe in the image of the triumphant, emancipated *beurette*; they knew they were subject to the same racism as the men. If the headscarf provoked such strong, apparently disproportionate reactions, it was because it was itself such a strong message, a nightmare called 'the return of the repressed'.

Such were the boomerang effects of French society's blatant discrimination against these women. The headscarf tells this society: 'You have marginalized us and penned us in, you tell us we're different, well, look: now we *are* different.' The 'veiled' woman is the alien landing in our midst. But this alien does not only challenge the 'French integration model'. This alien causes such malaise because her mere presence suddenly makes us see so-called 'sexual liberation' for what it is: the obligation for every woman to be 'desirable' at each and every moment. And women wearing the headscarf contravene this obligation. As Samira Bellil remarked in an interview a few months before her death, some men's obsession with veiling us is only equalled by other men's obsession with stripping us naked. These two obsessions are two symmetrical forms of one and the same negation of women: one wants women to arouse men's desires all the time, while the other forbids them from doing so. But in both cases the reference point for women's thinking and bodies is men's desire. The headscarf unveils the fact that in our supposedly liberated epoch, a woman's body is still not hers and hers alone.

Moreover, this alien makes Islam visible. Which the Franco-French can't stand.

Islam has only ever been tolerated in France on condition that it is discreet, preferably underground. And now these people are proud of it! There's something that defies sense here

– the dominant common sense, anyway. We saw the same incredulous outraged reactions over gay pride.

Domination is based on tolerance, which is the opposite of acceptance: that is, it rests on the idea that the practices or the very existence – or both – of the dominated, of the gay and lesbian, of the Muslim, are bad. But we let them exist all the same, so long as they admit that they're in the wrong. And the proof that they admit it is that they're ashamed. And the proof that they're ashamed is that they hide. So when the dominated no longer hide, asserting that their existence or their practices are the equal of anyone else's, they are trashing the rules of the game, breaking the contract that allows them to exist in the shadow of the dominant. So these latter have no other choice but to pull them back into line, putting them back in their place and showing them who's boss.[23] That's what France did with the headscarf law.

However, the headscarf is just one skirmish in the war against Arabs, Africans and Muslims. The local system of domination – France's caste system – is now compounded by its participation in a global project: the 'war on terror', which is in fact a war against the Arab and Muslim world. The partisans of the anti-headscarf law deftly linked the question of adolescents wearing the veil to the threat of al-Qaeda terrorism. French racism, without which these castes could not work, was thus strengthened by the myth of the dangers that the Muslim world posed. These attacks on the Arab and Muslim world are not new: for a long time Western essayists have been denouncing it as intrinsically incompatible with democracy, human rights, modernity, etc. In the 1970s, Bernard Lewis presented his theory of a clash of civilizations, though only with Samuel Huntington's version did it really 'take off'.[24]

23 See Chapter 3.
24 Alain Gresh, *L'Islam, la République et le monde*, Paris: Fayard,

In continuity with its support for the State of Israel's policy of expansion, from the 1990s onward the United States launched a series of attacks: the first Gulf War, Afghanistan, Iraq again, and so on.

France did participate, whatever its assertions to the contrary, in this enterprise of destruction and large-scale massacres of civilians. And domestically it benefited from its rhetoric. After all, there were plenty of advantages to be had from creating a climate in France where every Arab is seen as a Muslim, every Muslim as a fundamentalist and every Arab as a potential terrorist. Indeed, when Arabs are accused of being the fifth column in an international plot, and when they are attacked all day long for supposedly planning to replace Western civil codes with sharia,[25] it becomes almost impossible to recognize them as victims of racism. We can't treat them as a domestic enemy and at the same time carry out positive actions to their benefit. France thus has some more breathing space to not put an end to its caste system, for the moment at least.

Act III: repression
Thus the veil affair opened the third act of this French tragedy: after the first act (oppression) came the second act (rebellion); and the third act is the repression of this rebellion.

There is a striking parallel between this repression of protests against injustice in France and the United States' war without end after 9/11. Never asking itself any questions about its own responsibilities and the wrongs it has itself perpetrated, the West everywhere reacts to protests against the injustice it causes by aggravating the situation. It rejects dialogue and negotiation, always instead choosing intimidation

---

2004.
25   Corinne Lepage, 'Retrouver les valeurs républicaines', ResPublica. org.uk, 23 April 2004.

and exemplary punishment. However, we could have imagined the third act turning out differently, very differently. We could have hoped that France would regain control of its senses, recognizing its past and present wrongs against immigrants and their children, starting to redress these wrongs and deciding to eliminate racial discrimination; we could have hoped that it would finally get down to dismantling the patriarchal system rather than denying its existence; that it would put its own house in order rather than preaching to others; that it would stop setting women against the children of immigrants, and vice versa; in short, that it would finally adopt the path of equality, having already proclaimed it on the frontispieces of its town halls for some two hundred years. Can we still hope for or even imagine this happening? That's the key question. Even if the third act is off to a bad start, the play is still not over yet. The future will tell us if we are headed toward the consolidation of the caste system or its disappearance.

But this question will not be resolved on French territory alone; for it is connected to the US war against the Arab and Muslim world. And we shouldn't neglect the irrational or affective elements of France's little war against the headscarf, nor of America's big war: we are Westerners, and as Sophie Bessis tells us, the West's culture is a 'culture of supremacy'.[26] This culture is reminiscent of the madness that the Greek gods inflicted on those they wanted to destroy. It is the origin of the double standards that the rest of the world criticizes the West for, and it is the reason why rather than righting this wrong the West stubbornly presses on, aggravating its own situation. The spiral of oppression, revolt and repression is constantly accelerating and taking on ever-larger dimensions.

Faced with this whirlwind, for the moment at least the oppressed's capacity to resist is weakened. One may fear that

---

26 Sophie Bessis, *L'Occident et les autres*, Paris: La Découverte, 2003.

their patience is at an end, and that they will lose hope in the effectiveness of peaceful and legal protests when they see the barrier represented by the West's combination of immoderation, irresponsibility, arrogance and the desire to dominate – in short, its hubris – in its current relations with the rest of the world.

CHAPTER 9

A Movement: What Movement?

The *indigènes*[1] movement was born with the march of the *indigènes*,[2] even before it met formally. This is the movement of those who recognize themselves in the term *indigènes*. This self-recognition as *indigènes* is far from just intuitive: and those men and women who have done so have clearly already made a step that is important both psychologically and politically, expressing a new understanding of their situation. The fact that they call themselves *indigènes* shows that they are aware of their objective place in French society; and that they're not trying to remedy it by denying that it exists, as in the incessant appeals to the letter of French republicanism – 'We're French like you'. They know that the white other is really thinking, 'No, you're not like us'.

This has created an unprecedented situation in France: one that most non-*indigènes* consider dangerous. For, one of the main bases of domination is everyone keeping quiet about things that everyone knows to be true. Thus in the accepted formula 'We're French like you' – which the *indigènes* previously attempted to use, in order to appeal to whites' noble

---

1 '*Indigène*' was the inferior legal status that the French Empire attributed to its native colonial subjects. In 2005 an anti-racist movement, 'Les indigènes de la République', was launched with an *Appeal*, its name both invoking this history of oppression and recuperating this badge of indigenous identity – *translator's note*.

2 Christine Delphy, 'Une affaire française', in Charlotte Nordmann (ed.), *Le Foulard islamique en questions*, Paris: Amsterdam, 2004, pp. 64–72. See also the chapter 'Race, class and gender in France' above.

sentiments and thus put an end to discrimination – the unspoken part – 'and we know that you don't think that' – is just as important as the part that is spoken. But domination requires communication being established on the base of the law alone: principles, that is, not reality. The dominated always have to repeat the law, the official rule, even when they know – and the others know that they know – that it is not only empty, but the very opposite of the real situation. They have to say what the official rules are. But in so doing, they are also unknowingly saying that the law is more powerful and more important than anything else: that words count for more than deeds, and rhetoric for more than reality. This is why the *indigènes* are required to repeat what the law is, before they can say anything else. For this blunts any critique that they might then make: once the rule has been invoked, reality looks like a 'non-application of the law', which is by definition less important than the rule itself. And so 'non-application of the law' can prosper. In the end, this non-application is the rule itself: what I'll call 'the real rule'.

Everything changes when we say that it isn't a question of the 'non-application of the law' – a term that implies an 'accident' or something 'malfunctioning'. When we say that there is another unspoken rule, counter to the official rule, and which is the rule that is applied and operative in reality, this other rule is the real rule.

This is what the *indigènes* are saying: 'It's not that we're French people like any other who happen to fall victim to racist miscreants here and there; rather, we are one of the two categories resulting from the real rule, which establishes who are the real French – and the real humans – and who are the false French and the false humans. It creates the former by creating the latter'.

And some people are scandalized by the *indigènes*. The scandal is not the fact that the emperor has no clothes, but that someone dares say it; the scandal is not that the official rule isn't the one that works in practice – governing people's behaviour – but that someone dares to say it. Because pretending that there is just one rule and that it is applied in practice is the condition of the real rule's survival.

The *indigènes* have changed the rules of the game. They have transgressed the rule that we must not lift the veil from the real rule, or better, that we must always pretend that we aren't aware of it, thus allowing it to play out in the full freedom of the world of the 'non-existent'.

To mention the real rule is to pass a point of no return, because it breaks with the rule of the game, which demands that we believe or at least pretend to believe that the official rule is the real one. The official rule includes not just its own substance but also this other rule regarding how it is to be used, this rule of the game.

And this rupture with the consensus view is not without its consequences: this point of no return is also a political position. Most of the groups who fight against discrimination do so within the legal framework of the official rule – everyone has to – but also within the discursive, analytical, theoretical and political framework of this official rule, which demands that we do not lift the veil from the fact that it's not the real rule.

The *indigènes'* political position on the official rule – which, they openly declare, is not the real rule – will also provide the basis for their position with regard to groups that have the same ultimate objectives but that accept the rule of the game, which is that the official rules are real, and one should not point to their fictitious character.

Practically speaking, does this mean a change of alliances? Yes, in my view. Indeed, it will transform the political landscape, and it is already doing so. Political groups and associations fighting discrimination will be tempted to define themselves by either separating from us or drawing closer to what we are doing, namely uncovering the non-reality of the official rule and breaking with the rule of the game. And lifting this veil means revisiting our analysis of French society.

After all, if the official rule is not the real rule, then what does the latter consist of? What is the content of the real rule? When we take the lid off the consensus over what the rule is, what comes out of Aladdin's lamp? What does French society look like after we've denounced the rule of the game, which is to pretend not to see the unreality of the official rule?

The question at this point is not so much – or is no longer – a matter of talking about what remains of colonialism or racism. These questions belong to a previous time, when we took the official rule for the real one. The question now posed concerns at what point these 'remains' come to transform the vision that we might have had of contemporary society, and what is the significance of the real rule as compared to the official rule. More broadly, what relation is there between reality (the real rule) and fiction (the official rule)? Does the official rule do anything other than hide the real one? Does it regulate anything other than this need to hide the real rule?

Everyone knows that this is a crucial moment, and it's this that explains the violent reaction that greeted us: we posed the question of what should define – and what already defines – French society. Is it primarily defined by equality; an equality that although 'sullied by malfunctions' remains both the official *and* real rule, mistakes and exceptions notwithstanding? Or is the real rule inequality – the inequality of 'races', classes and 'sexes'?

1. Lest we forget, with this appeal we first of all produced an analysis that went against all the rules of this society's discourse about itself. Obviously we are not in any sense constrained by the appeal. But for now it would be a good idea

to stick to a few of its key ideas. These tell us that French society is not 'sometimes, accidentally, unknowingly' unequal and discriminatory, but that it is founded on inequality and discrimination and a clear hierarchy of groups, with white, bourgeois, heterosexual men at the top. And this hierarchy does matter, *pace* our far-Left friends who, though considering class divisions to be the system's *modus operandi* rather than a case of it malfunctioning, nonetheless also believe that racial divisions are such a disorder, or a 'consequence' of class divisions – in short, not seeing them as a specific and thus at least partially autonomous system.

The appeal said that the racial or 'white/*indigène*' division is not an unhappy coincidence, but rather a structural characteristic of society, just as structural as class division. It embodies a principle of division and hierarchy that cannot simply be dissolved in the 'social question'.

This disagreement on the analytical plane inevitably produced a clash on the political terrain.

2. The specificity of each oppression is the basis for the autonomy of each struggle, but even an autonomous struggle must address the way in which oppressions overlap – this being synonymous with social divisions. The appeal's analysis, whether explicit or implicit, attributed equal importance to both racial and class divides. It furthermore insisted that analysis of class divisions should be adapted in order to account for racial divisions. This theoretical and political concern has long existed in other countries, and there are many analyses of the articulation of these two systems. Here isn't the place to expand on this point and compare the two systems; what we will say is that our society cannot go on much longer neglecting this theoretical and political question.

However, the appeal did fail to attribute equal importance to the gender divide.

This is not a surprise. In spite of appeals to unity, unity does not thrive at the moment. We can ask how such unity could be realized in conditions where hierarchical social divisions were not stacked one on top of another. In any case, if they weren't, we wouldn't be speaking of *divisions* in the plural.

And concretely: with the appeal, and before that with the headscarf controversy, we saw the groups most critical of reality and the workings of the official rule – leftists (who think that the real structuring principle is class division) and some feminists (who think that the gender divide prevails over the system's supposed universalism) – becoming republicans again; indeed, when they defended 'the bill' they became 'national', not to say nationalists. Suddenly they saw the virtues of the parliamentary democracy they had long denounced. Why? Each group views reality through the prism of its own oppression, which it sees as the most important of the effective rules of social hierarchy. But when it comes to the other oppressions, each group *de facto* adopts the 'official' analysis that these are cases of the system malfunctioning.

This makes alliances difficult. But in my view the problem isn't the autonomy of each struggle. If there were autonomous struggles on every terrain of each oppression, this would establish a relation of forces – a balance – that would force each of these struggles to account for the struggles waged by others, and thus for the oppression that they suffer. The problem comes when each group claims to take a global view, when in fact its own oppression is magnified while the others are minimized.

So there are two types of tension:

a) On the one hand, tensions between

– the autonomy of struggles, which is absolutely necessary, insofar as every struggle must be based on the experience of a real and concrete oppression; and, indeed, each group must analyse its own oppression before it can even imagine putting it together with other people's;

– a global vision of society and oppressions, which each group must have, or else implicitly does have. Unfortunately, the most global vision is also the most globalizing one – 'all together now', a disembodied vision where some people claim to speak in the name of everyone and everything, when they in fact speak for no one and nothing. This is the present-day function of the expression 'the class struggle', discreetly rebaptized the 'social question'. These words do not denote a reality on the ground; rather, they are a magic formula that allows the real struggles of real people against real oppressions to be termed 'corporatist' and 'divisive'. Groups who have appointed themselves the leaders of all struggles wield this weapon of intellectual terrorism; they have long presented themselves as such a leadership, and persist in this pretention despite their patent failure to lead or even to give some impulse to any struggles at all.

So there can be no *a priori* 'all together now' before each struggle has asserted itself and the others have recognized its legitimacy.

b) But on the other hand, there are also *internal* tensions within each struggle. Oppressions are multiple rather than all integrated into one; but nor are they lined up in separate columns. That's too simplistic. Even if we just take the example of the *indigènes*, this isn't a group of women who suffer 'sex'/gender oppression and nothing else standing next to men who suffer racial oppression and nothing else. Rather, we have women who are dominated both as *indigènes* and women, and men who are dominated for being *indigènes* and yet are dominant in terms of their 'sex'/gender. (And moreover, the *indigènes* are not homogeneous in terms of their social class; I'll leave this question aside for the moment, but this group is indeed traversed by class antagonisms.)

The rejection of an *a priori* 'all together now' and the affirmation of difference will not resolve this problem. This is a major challenge. However easily we can refute the accusation of 'dividing the working class' (particularly when this charge is levelled by petty-bourgeois without a leg to stand on) the accusation of dividing the *indigène* movement will come up very quickly, as soon as women *indigènes* argue that the situation of the 'typical' *indigène* is in fact that of a male one; and as soon as the question of what is 'universal', 'general' and 'defining' about this situation is re-examined through the lens of gender. And we will thus be forced to recognize that here as elsewhere, universalism conceals the particular interests of the dominant.

Conclusion

So we see that the convergence of struggles in the future will pose the same questions as are today posed (or must be posed) when we discuss the autonomy of different struggles. After all, no group – *indigènes* any more than women – is homogeneous. There are women who are dominant from a 'racial' point of view; among the *indigènes* some belong to the dominant gender; and conversely there are racially dominated women and *indigènes* dominated on account of their gender. The questions have long been studied in the English-speaking world, where they always speak in terms of the three words 'gender, race and class'. It is difficult to take them all into account simultaneously, but it is nonetheless necessary to do so. It leads to different recompositions of and variations on the analysis of each of these major categories, but also results in different political alliances.

Should we consider these contradictions, these dominations,

as internal to any kind of category – be it 'founded' on 'sex', 'race' or 'class'? Or should we reject these categories in favour of basing ourselves on the situation of real people, who never belong to one category alone and are always – or almost always – dominated in one category and dominant in another?

We have no easy answers to that question. Certainly, however, people have changed the content of gender, racial and class analysis on the basis of their own real situation of double or multiple oppressions – for example, poor black women in the Americas. At the same time, it would be counter-productive to totally abandon these categories on the basis that real people always exist in the spaces where multiple categories overlap. For these categories are not without meaning, and their identification and analysis does mark a theoretical and political advance; they point to the structures of oppression and are useful for helping people analyse their own situation, even if they then realize that they are also oppressed by other systems. Simply to note the multiplicity of individual positions produced by the overlapping of these three great variables would lead to ever more numerous segmentations and would ultimately make each and every individual a political struggle unto her/himself alone; and a struggle has to be collective. Taking the variety of oppressions and their combinations into account is not the same thing as returning to the isolation of individuals in their unique, incomparable existence.

In its broad mechanisms, racial oppression is comparable to gender oppression. However, each of these constitutes a specific oppression. Indeed, while racial oppression does not bring together a population who are all oppressed in one homogeneous way, it does nonetheless bring together a specific population that includes people from *both* the dominant *and* the dominated sides of gender oppression – this population being the *indigènes*.

In turn, gender oppression brings together a population including people from *both* the dominant *and* the dominated sides of racial oppression – this population being women. These different dividing lines show that each of these oppressions is specific and cannot be blended into the other.

So we ought to think about the specificity of 'racial' oppression, the oppression of *indigènes*. We forget at our own peril the fact that this population is *brought together* by one oppression and also *divided* by another. It's not that we are dividing it, or will divide it: it is always-already divided. That is why I believe that struggling against gender oppression within this group *and right away* is no bonus option, but rather the *sine qua non* condition for any effective struggle.

CHAPTER 10

Anti-sexism or Anti-racism?
A False Dilemma

This article, which follows a number of essays on the 'Islamic headscarf', does not address the many aspects of the French legislation banning state-school pupils from wearing the veil. We will read with interest the chapters that Alain Gresh[1] and Oliver Roy[2] devote to the history of this bill, in particular in terms of French secularism [*laïcité*] and the fabrication of an 'Islamic threat' in these last two decades, serving to legitimize this law. The identification of the headscarf as a problem – organized by the protagonists of French political life[3] – proceeded through two decisive phases of 'extracting' public consent. Firstly, a process of criminalizing 'Muslims',[4] transmitted by media who gave this whole affair disproportionate prominence – indeed, twice as much as the dismantling of Social Security. Secondly, the controversy, the debate, its conclusion and its aftershocks were inscribed in a wider dynamic, namely an Islamophobia that took over the reins from

---

1   Alain Gresh, *L'Islam, la République et le monde*, Paris: Fayard, 2004.

2   Olivier Roy, *La Laïcité face à l'islam*, Paris: Stock, 2005.

3   Françoise Lorcerie, 'À l'assaut de l'agenda public: la politisation du voile islamique en 2003–2004', in *La Politisation du voile*, Paris: l'Harmattan, 2005. Fabienne Brion, 'L'inscription du débat français en Belgique: pudeurs laïques et monnaie de singe', in F. Lorcerie (ed.), *La Politisation du voile*.

4   Pierre Tevanian, *Le Voile médiatique. Un faux débat: 'l'affaire du foulard islamique'*, Paris: Raisons d'agir, 2005.

anti-Arab racism,[5] and which also met with media support, constructing an imaginary, dangerous view of Islam.[6] According to Saïd Bouamama,[7] the anti-headscarf law and the new Islamophobia have the goal of ethnicizing the social problems created by discrimination, and to this end, making racism 'respectable'. In 'Race, Caste and Gender in France'[8] I interpreted this law as a sign of French society's rejection of French men and women who are the descendants of former colonial subjects, in response to their demand for full citizenship. Most of the authors I cited criticized the interpretation of the headscarf that was used to justify its banning – the idea that it symbolizes an inferiority which the women who wear it accept. Instead they emphasized the many contrary meanings already discussed by Françoise Gaspard and Farad Khosrokhavar in 1995,[9] in particular its significance as a protest in the face of racism, 'turning the stigma around'. This phenomenon was already well known to sociologists ever since the first pioneering works on American symbolic interactionism.[10]

So here I do not want to discuss the 'pros' and 'cons' of the law – that's been done already – but rather to examine the 'feminist' arguments that were used, invoking women's rights. These were almost entirely absent from the 1989 debate and yet now constitute the essential substance of the case for this

---

5   Vincent Geisser, *La Nouvelle Islamophobie*, Paris: La Découverte, 2003.

6   Thomas Deltombe, *L'Islam imaginaire. La construction médiatique de l'islamophobie en France, 1975–2005*, Paris: La Découverte, 2005.

7   Saïd Bouamama, *L'Affaire du foulard islamique: la production d'un racisme respectable*, Paris: Le Geai bleu, 2004.

8   See Chapter 8 in this volume.

9   Françoise Gaspard and Farad Khosrokhavar, *Le Foulard et la République*, Paris: La Découverte, 1995.

10   Erving Goffmann, *Stigmata: Notes on the Management of Spoiled Identity*, Englewood Cliffs, NJ: Prentice-Hall, 1964; Howard Saul Becker, *Outsiders*, London: Free Press of Glencoe, 1963.

legislation. How come a law that was presented as a matter of '*laïcité*' was ultimately debated principally in terms of women's rights (even though there's no trace of this in the text of the legislation)? It's because the secularist argument was weak and they needed to find another. Equality between the sexes . . . yes, that'll do. Indeed, we witnessed the spectacle – whether you found it amusing or lamentable – of party leaders, ministers, the prime minister, the President of the Republic, all of them men, raging about the 'hole' that the headscarf had torn in equality between the sexes; and this equality was suddenly presented as one of the pillars if not *the* pillar of the Republic, its existence suddenly having become incontestable. The question had never crossed their minds before, but suddenly, in winter 2003, equality between women and men became their number one priority, their constant concern. And a handful of teenage women wearing the headscarf became the only obstacle to this equality in all of France.

Even if the feminist movement didn't begin this controversy, given that women's rights were recruited to serve in the frontline of the debate we might have thought that this movement would be somehow involved. But it wasn't at all. The Stasi commission (appointed in Autumn 2003 by Jacques Chirac, at that time president) did not hear submissions from any feminists – and it was this commission's final report that legitimized the law. The government representative theoretically responsible for this question – the secretary of state for equality and parity – did not contribute to the commission either, and did not ask to be heard. Moreover, the feminist movement had never demanded or encouraged such legislation. Feminists in France do not have the power to initiate such a far-reaching affair, or even a smaller one; and even when it comes to much more serious subjects like male violence against women, they don't manage to capture the attentions of politicians or the media.

But they do have things to say about the 'feminist' arguments called up by (non-feminist) politicians in order to justify the law – 'sexism', 'equality between the sexes', 'oppression', 'women's inferior status', etc. Indeed, they have addressed all these points. And it is precisely because feminists have picked up on these themes that we are interested in analysing such arguments.

The law divided feminists, just as it divided all political groups to the left of the Parti Socialiste. Many feminists came out in support of the bill, a few against, but many fell silent, undecided and often taken aback by it all. So yes, I will examine the arguments used by the feminists who stated their support for the law. But I will also address the reasoning of those who remained stuck at the crossroads, troubled by the fact that on the one hand the law was meant to protect young Muslim girls from family constraints forcing them to wear the headscarf *and yet* on the other hand it is a discriminatory law stigmatizing a whole population. This *and yet* is the issue here. More than one feminist had the painful feeling of facing an impossible dilemma, that is, having to choose to sacrifice either the victims of sexism or the victims of racism. More than one feminist refused to decide, shutting themselves away in silence. So here we want to understand the content of this heartfelt dilemma: did we have to choose between two sets of victims? Between the anti-sexist struggle and the anti-racist struggle?

And if that is the case, then *is it the way the questions were asked, the way the 'problem' was stated, which led to this dilemma?* I will try to demonstrate that this dilemma is based on false assumptions.

I will also try and draw some theoretical and practical consequences from my examination of this false dilemma. I will do so by posing the question of what kind of conceptualization of patriarchal (gender) oppression and racist oppression will allow feminism in France and the West more generally to avoid repeating the same error it attacks patriarchy for: namely, setting up a particular situation (men's situation) as a 'universal' and then counterposing this to another particular situation (women's). How can we avoid feminists – who like all women are victims of this false universalism – in turn coining their own 'ethno-centric universalism'[11] and opposing this to (and imposing it on) other dominated groups?

The feminist arguments in favour of banning the headscarf
The pro-ban feminists' arguments were politicians' arguments. They were formulated as early as 1989 by Élisabeth Badinter, Régis Debray, Alain Finkielkraut, Élisabeth de Fontenay and Catherine Kintzler. Ten years later, a *Libération* column revisited these arguments and gave them further precision; it was signed by Gaye Petek and Alain Seksig,[12] who were later appointed members of the Stasi commission. The first text began with the consideration that the legal protection for freedom of religious expression is an inadmissible show of permissiveness: '*Tolerating* the Islamic headscarf . . . means holding the door wide open to those who have decided once and for all and without discussion that Muslim women must do as they say . . . In giving *de facto* authorization to the Islamic headscarf, a symbol of women's submission, you are giving free rein to their fathers and brothers, that is, *the harshest patriarchy on the planet.*'[13] Meanwhile in the second piece we can see all the themes that would later serve as arguments for the law, in the Stasi commission as well as among

11 Chandra Tapalde Mohanty, 'Under Western Eyes: Feminist Scholarship and Colonial Discourses', in *Feminism without Borders*, Durham, NC: Duke University Press, 2004, p. 21.

12 On 12 November 1999.

13 'Profs, ne capitulons pas!', appeal signed by five intellectuals, *Le Nouvel Observateur*, 1304, 2–8 November 1989.

the pro-ban feminists. As Lorcerie noted,[14] the content of what the head of state presented as the consensus had already been drawn up five years previously.

Following the (right-wing) fleet

This was the programme debated at the Stasi commission, which included the following main points: the headscarf is a political-religious symbol; it is discriminatory and draws attention to who is and who isn't wearing it; the high-school students who insist on wearing it exclude themselves; religious symbols have to be discreet, and faith a private matter; it's advisable to ban all conspicuous religious symbols, even the kippah (a concession that had so far been refused by representatives of the Jewish community); it is not a question of stigmatizing Islam and Muslim populations, but of the fight against fundamentalism. France and Algeria, one struggle;[15] we need a law putting secularism back into the classroom; no to the Conseil d'État's version of secularism, which would allow veiled students' parents to have their way.

---

14   Françoise Lorcerie, 'À l'assaut de l'agenda public: la politisation du voile islamique en 2003–2004' in F. Lorcerie, *La politisation du voile*, Paris; L'Harmattan, 2005.

15   In 1991 the first round of the Algerian parliamentary elections suggested victory for the Islamic Salvation Front (FIS). The army cancelled the second round. In the parties, unions and women's association there was growing division between those who approved of the military coup countering the Islamist threat – who soon came to be known as the 'eradicators' – and the partisans of 'dialogue' who rejected the coup. The Algerian authorities arrested the Islamists en masse; others took to maquis fighting. The civil war that followed was a terrible mess of a situation: a 'dirty war', where all the armed groups took the population hostage. Certain 'eradicators' – some of whom took refuge in France – were among the most fervent supporters of banning the veil in France, arguing that 'if we allow the headscarf today, tomorrow the Islamists will reach power by the ballot box like in Algeria, and civil war will follow'. However unlikely all this sounds, the supporters of the ban used this fantasy in order to confer a dramatic aspect on France's headscarf affair.

That said, these arguments were not all used by all the pro-ban feminists, publicly at least. Some of them were more of a consensus view and were widely used, while others only appeared in individual columns or texts published online.

The headscarf as a symbol of the oppression of women

The idea that the headscarf symbolizes women's submission was the foremost argument put forward by feminists as well as the career politicians. Historically speaking, in the Mediterranean and the Middle East the obligation for women to cover their heads is certainly a marker of men's domination of women, mentioned in the three 'religions of the Book' that have developed in these regions. But during the debate in France preceding the bill's writing into law, it acquired a peculiar status: it became the *only* sign of the oppression of women. The pro-ban feminists do not even attribute so much importance to the denuding of women promoted by pseudo-'sexual liberation' (in fact a Western, masculine conception of it) and the commodification of women's bodies. Michèle Dayras, president of SOS-Sexisme and a partisan of the bill, wrote in her 'Ni à poil, ni en voile!' ['Neither in the buff nor veiled!'] that 'women have to answer a thousand demands on what they wear, the ultimate goal of which is seduction: showing off more flesh or hiding it all. You'd think there was nothing more to women's existence than their status as sex objects!'[16] Here she draws a parallel between the injunction to reveal the body and to cover it up: equally designed for men, equally compulsory . . . equally oppressive? No. She mentions the two extremes for the sake of taking a position in between, and not at all in order to suggest that they are equivalents. The repeated mention of the thong as an over-the-top expression of the wish to

16 'Ni à poil, ni en voile!', 3 February 2003, published on the EF-L e-list, 3 November 2004.

seduce by showing off the body – comparable to the wish to seduce by concealing it with a veil – does not establish any symmetry between the two: after all, no one is saying that the thong ought to be banned. The headscarf is considered incomparably worse than any other symbol.

Nor is any comparison made with the specific markers of Western femininity: high heels, lipstick, or make-up in general. Yet the feminist movement of the 1970s denounced these in the same terms in which the headscarf is attacked today, as a form of alienation imposed on women.

Nor are we allowed to discuss what the women who wear the headscarf think it means. Yet the critiques that feminists have made of the hyper-sexualisation of Western life can also help explain why these women have taken this path. No one makes the argument that perhaps they, too, proceed on the basis of these same critiques; it's taken as read, *a priori*, that their motivations can't have anything to do with our own, as by definition they are foreign. In every sense, the very possibility of discussion with women who wear the headscarf is expressly ruled out, since whatever meaning these women might attribute to their actions, it isn't worth taking into consideration. Rather, the headscarf has a 'universal' meaning, which only Western feminists are able to discern. Such is the position of the Collectif national des droits des femmes (CNDF).[17] Like the Stasi commission, which refused on principle to give a hearing to 'veiled' girls, the CNDF refused them entry to its meetings and tried to stop them participating in the 8 March [International Women's Day] demonstrations in 2004 and 2005, the November 2004 march protesting violence

---

17   The CNDF is a major coalition bringing together feminist associations and the majority of left-wing parties and unions (with 150 nominal collaborators). The history of the CNDF's adoption of a pro-ban position is very interesting, but it would require too much space to deal with here.

against women and the January 2005 rally to mark thirty years since the decriminalization of abortion. So for these feminists the headscarf is not only *the* symbol of women's submission; it has come to symbolize the idea that the women who wear it, and all those who refuse to exclude them, are unworthy of fighting for women's rights.

'First the veil – then comes rape'

Once the veil is ascribed this 'universal' meaning, all sorts of interpretative elisions and amalgams become possible. Thus the discourse favouring the ban very strongly associated the headscarf with the sexist violence that takes place 'in the ghettos'; it is the consequence of this violence – women protect themselves from rape by covering up – but also its cause – rapists pick out their prey by seeing who isn't wearing it. Liliane Kandel wrote, 'The fact that some women do submit (or agree) [to wearing the headscarf] also means that those who refuse to do so are systematically harassed and treated as "whores" – or raped'.[18] Not only does she refuse the headscarf as a symbol of submission, but she sees the women who wear it as rapists' willing accomplices, because without them the rapists wouldn't know exactly who to rape. Is she sure that banning headscarves would be enough to stop rape? However absurd and hateful this allegation, no one among the bill's partisans thought it worth distancing themselves from it.

In short, the headscarf also became the symbol of sexist violence. Not sexist violence in general, but a sexist violence specific to the ghettos and the populations who live there. The headscarf was presented as symbolizing the existence of 'another' culture in France characterized by 'another' sexism, different to 'ordinary' French sexism (and some, Élisabeth

---

18 Liliane Kandel, 'Un foulard qui provoque d'étranges cécités', *Le Monde*, 8 July 2003.

Badinter[19] prominent among them, questioned whether this latter really exists at all). In her *Le Monde* article mentioned above, Kandel stuck closely to this line of argument: she reckoned that to claim that 'sexism is everywhere', as feminists have always said, is 'a ridiculous, blind attitude'.

So what is this culture, founded on male supremacy and characterized by rape? It's 'Muslim' culture: and women's oppression is held to be a fundamental principle of this culture, to the point that some feminists end up imagining an essential identity between the headscarf and criminality. In the words of Élise Thiébaut, a journalist at *Clara Magazine* – organ of Femmes Solidaires, formerly the Communist Party's Union des femmes françaises: 'We can delve into the whys and wherefores of this "youth neo-Islamism". But faced with the rise of extremisms, we have other duties beyond simply explaining this. We must also find the means to counter it. We can discuss for the rest of our days "why is there rape?", "why is there oppression?", or "why me?" This is important, but it's not enough . . . when we talk about the veil, we're talking about rape.'[20]

From Muslim rape to the 'Islamic threat'
Like the Stasi commission, these feminists directly linked the 'global Islamic threat' to the 'culture' that today exists (or always existed) in the ghettos where the descendants of immigrants live. In its 'soft' version this Islamic plot is a national

---

19   'The onset of the third millennium will coincide with an extraordinary reversal of the relations of force. Not only will the patriarchal system be dead and buried across most of the industrialized West, but we will see a new imbalance, this time to the exclusive benefit of women', Élisabeth Badinter, 'Une prospective pour l'an 2000', in Yolande Cohen (ed.), *Femmes et contre-pouvoirs*, Paris: Boréal, 1987.

20   'Tous voiles dehors', 11 November 2003, http://sisyphe.org/article. php3?id _article=761.

one, seeking to demand special dispensations for Muslims. At a 5 February 2004 meeting of the Coordination féministe et laïque, the former Socialist women's rights minister Yvette Roudy declared that '[The veil affair] is very much part of an intimidation strategy being waged by a Muslim fundamentalist current determined to set the precepts of their religion above the laws of the Republic ... Bringing the veil into the school is an act of defiance against the Republic, instigated by fundamentalists.'[21]

Take this one step further, and the Islamists' supposed objective becomes control over the whole 'possibly' Muslim population. The idea that a 'plot' is under way is expanded into the allegation that the Islamists – whether French nationals or otherwise – want to impose Islamic law on the whole country. That same evening, Corinne Lepage, the former (conservative) environment minister, declared that 'without doubt, battle has been joined between those who would have France change its republican laws and traditions to make it possible to apply sharia, and those who want the republican principle to prevail, fighting . . . for a consistent application of the principle of secularism [*laïcité*] and the equality of men's and women's rights in all fields'.[22]

In its 'hard' version, the headscarf is just 'the tip of the iceberg' (as the expression used during the debate had it) of the war that the joint forces of al-Qaeda and the UOIF[23] have declared against the entire Western world. Kandel decries the blindness of those who imagine that 'the fundamentalist threat, like the clouds from Chernobyl, stops at the French border'.

---

21 Yvette Roudy, 11 January 2004, http://sisyphe.org/article. ph3?id_article=885.

22 *Respublica*: www.gaucherepublicaine.org.

23 L'Union des Organisations Islamiques de France – *translator's note*.

So the pro-ban feminists re-used almost all the arguments made in favour of legislation in the Stasi commission, with the exception of the accusation of anti-Semitism levelled against young 'Beurs' [children of North African immigrants], notably by Stasi commission rapporteur Rémy Schwartz.[24] But this accusation is so integral to Huntington's theory of a 'clash of civilizations' that it is always in the background of any version of this theory. So just like the 'women's rights' arguments used at the Stasi commission and in the whole of the media, those redeployed by pro-ban feminists cannot be understood except in the context of the omnipresent discourse, whether explicit or implicit, of the 'Islamic threat'.[25]

The 'international' headscarf: dubious comparisons and the instrumentalisation of feminist campaigns

Like the Stasi commission, the media, publishers and finally France as a whole, pro-ban feminists often made recourse to international comparisons. Such comparisons were very selective. For the ban on the headscarf (called, not inadvertently, the 'veil') to be considered an urgent matter of national concern and for its human cost – excluding girls from school – to seem justified in light of the potential danger, it was necessary to create a certain media climate. Namely, one in which parallels could plausibly be drawn between radically different national scenarios with problems of wholly dissimilar nature and order of magnitude.

---

24 Alain Gresh, *L'Islam la république et le monde*, p. 314.

25 'The meaning of this "Islamic threat" is never truly defined. Who is it describing? Groups like al-Qaeda, with their blind, murderous acts against civilians? Islamist movements involved in legal activities? All Muslims? ... The question is whether these groups [terrorists like al-Qaeda] represent the whole political terrain of Islamism, and pose a "strategic" threat to the West of the likes of Nazism or communism' (Alain Gresh, *L'Islam, la république et le monde*, p. 114).

And very specific contexts were always invoked in support of this cause. That is, the countries where a full-body veil, the chador, has been imposed in law, particularly Iran, where a political police checks that women are indeed cloaked in this garment; and Algeria, where even before the civil war the Islamists tried to force women in the areas they controlled to wear the veil, sometimes by means of acid attacks. These examples were taken to be representative of the condition of all Arab and/or Muslim countries, allowing a further elision: everywhere that the veil is worn, it is forced on the women concerned through hideous violence. This was the arbitrary generalization allowing André Glucksmann to write that 'the veil is a terrorist operation. In France, zealous schoolgirls know that their veils are stained with blood.'[26] The constant invocation of Iran and Algeria and Chahdortt Djavann's[27] success in bookshops, on TV and at the Stasi commission propagated a miserabilist view of women in majority-Muslim countries: inevitably everywhere oppressed by Islam.

There are precedents for this image in contemporary French and Western feminist movements.[28] And if we take a look back we can see that international solidarity campaigns, above all those that circulated online, have mainly if not exclusively concerned women in majority-Muslim countries: the campaign over women's suffering under the Taliban, depriving them of the right to leave their homes not enveloped in burqas,

---

26 'Foulard. Le complot. Comment les islamistes nous infiltrent', *L'Express*, 17 November 1994.

27 An Iranian woman, living and writing in France, whose novels, delving into the horrors of the state-imposed and police-enforced veil, have met with great success.

28 There are also striking parallels between this outlook and the view that certain French feminists had of Algerian women in the nineteenth century (Julia Clancy-Smith, 'Le regard colonial: Islam, genre et identités dans la fabrication de l'Algérie française, 1830–1962', *Nouvelles Questions féministes*, 25/1, 2006).

then the right to work, and finally their right to enter hospitals; the campaign in solidarity with a number of women threatened with stoning in Niger; solidarity with Algerian feminists who have been denouncing that country's family code for some two decades.

All these campaigns were legitimate. The troubling thing is that taken together, their selectiveness could give the impression that women's oppression in non-Western countries is exclusively linked to Islam. Not so much what was said, but what was not said, biased the picture against Muslim countries. For example, in spite of the mass of documentation on the subject, FGM (female genital mutilation) – which is practised in Christian, animist and Muslim regions of Africa but is unknown in the majority of Muslim countries (North Africa, the Middle East [with the exception of Iraq], Indonesia, Malaysia) – is still largely attributed to Islam. The wife-burning perpetrated by husbands or parents in South Asia is more often associated with the 100 million Muslims in Pakistan than the one billion Hindus in India. And while we can't blame campaigns 'based on good intentions', nonetheless we must recognize that they have been instrumentalized by the great powers, and that we ought to have protested this instrumentalization much sooner. When Bush and Blair made the liberation of Afghan women their fourth reason for bombing Afghanistan in October 2001 – riding the wave of the international campaign against the treatment of Afghan women that had started three years previously – few feminists stood up to denounce this derailing of their campaign. Even more striking was feminists' silence following the 'liberation' of Kabul and then the rest of Afghanistan. Their interest in Afghan women suddenly vanished, and the vast majority of feminists simply stopped talking about them. Yet the mujahideens who replaced the Taliban were no more feminist than these latter had been, and the situation of Afghan women is perhaps even worse today than it was in 2001.[29]

We can also see that these international campaigns exclusively concern 'the South'. Well, the women of Belgium and Norway could certainly have done with our support, just as we need theirs. This is connected to a major problem in how we understand the world; and though it's not the work of feminists alone, it is a trap that we fall into with remarkable regularity. Namely, the idea that women's lot in the West is incontestably better than everywhere else.[30]

In France's headscarf affair, international comparisons served to take this garment out of its own political context and thus to ignore the specific social relations that structure French society: that is to say, caste relations whose ideological cover is inherited from colonialism. In accordance with this logic, the debate gave the impression that wherever the headscarf appeared, this would necessarily and inevitably soon lead to women being locked up in the home, forced marriages, stoning, FGM, the amputation of thieves' hands, etc. The headscarves worn by young French women were thus denounced not for what they are in the here and now, but for what they might herald. They were held to represent not what the women concerned think of them, but the entire array of detestable traits that the West chooses to emphasize in its demonization of Muslim countries and Islam. And this interpretation was imposed on the girls who wear it, who suddenly came to stand for the 'Orientalism' described by Edward Said. They were perceived as the sign that France is being invaded by 'Islam', as the 'clash of civilizations' theory

---

29   See above, 'A War for Afghan Women?'

30   Leti Volpp, 'Feminism versus Multiculturalism', *Columbia Law Review*, 101, 2001, p. 1198; Laura Nader, 'Orientalisme, occidentalisme et contrôle des femmes', *Nouvelles Questions féministes*, 25/1, 2006.

presents it – misogynist, anti-democratic, repressive, belli-
cose and cruel.

Extraordinary violence

The interpretative elisions in the pro-ban feminists' dubious
international comparisons have had numerous ideological
effects in France. Firstly, they have contributed to the systematic dissociation of the sexist violence perpetrated in the
ghettos from 'ordinary' sexist violence. This former is held up
as extraordinary: it's so much more serious that it's considered
in separation from ordinary violence, and never as an instance
of it. This extraordinary violence is then de-nationalized: the
'harshest patriarchy on the planet' could only come from outside the Hexagon; it is African and Muslim. In tandem with
this, the authors of this violence – blacks and Arabs – are
presented as standing outside of French society. In turn, the
foreignness of blacks' and Arabs' 'Muslim' (or 'African') violence is taken as proof that Islam is foreign, a slab that doesn't
fit into the pattern of French culture and society.

This othering process is compounded by the blackening of
the moral portrayal of men who are already often designated
by their skin colour. Blacks are 'black', and Arabs 'brown' or
'tanned' (and all of them 'darkies').

Anti-sexist and anti-racist struggles: compatible or counterposed?

This leads me to a question that has often been posed, and is
perhaps *the* question facing many of the feminists I mentioned
earlier who remained stuck at the crossroads. These feminists
were embarrassed and often silent, torn between their concern
for 'the fate of women in the ghettos' and their awareness that
the law could be considered racist. For them, the question was:
how can we confront the racism of this law without writing
off the problem of violence against women? This was a

question that troubled many. But its assumptions – 'not for-getting the violence against women in the ghettos' – show that the pro-ban discourse succeeded in promoting its principal message: namely, that there is extraordinary sexist violence in these ghettos. And the proof that it is extraordinary is that we have to think up an extraordinary, specific response to it. We thus take it for granted that it cannot be compared to and included in ordinary male violence. But these are one and the same. Male violence such as it manifests itself in the ghettos – sexist discrimination, harassment, intimidation, rape – is of the same order as the male violence that feminist organizations have always fought against. And the laws and policies devel-oped in opposition to this violence, however insufficient they may be, also apply to 'ghetto violence' (which has no need for this qualifier). If male violence in the ghettos is specific and different, or its victims are specific and different from other women, then it needs to be dealt with using specific and dif-ferent measures. But it is impossible to insist on specific measures without implying that the authors or victims of this violence are different from the 'ordinary' ones.

We have seen that for these feminists who found themselves 'torn', recognizing that the law is racist was not alone sufficient reason to oppose it. Hence they accepted the idea that laws could be good for women at the same time as being racist ('yes it's racist, perhaps, *but* don't forget women'). But could they accept the idea that laws targeting a particular population – racist laws – can nonetheless be anti-sexist, if they did not share the pro-ban feminists' fundamental premise that sexism is worse in the ghettos and thus merits special treatment?

Here we can make out the hallmark of a perspective telling us that the struggle against racism can stand in con-tradiction with the struggle against sexism, and vice versa. And if this question bugs so many feminists, it's because they think they have to make an agonizing choice: to them, the anti-racist struggle seems to *take away from* the anti-sexist struggle.

So before discussing the articulation of these struggles, we have to return to the question that gives rise to it: the articulation of oppressions. The mechanisms of the patriarchal (gender) system and the racist system are similar: assigning individuals to a social position on the basis of criteria that essentialize groups. But each system is based on different criteria, and it follows that these two systems construct two different sets of populations. The dilemma between anti-sexist and anti-racist struggle *only* makes sense if we suppose that the two populations targeted by racism and sexism are different. Well, racism certainly does construct two 'racial' groups, but each of these comprises two 'genders'; and the gender system does indeed construct two 'gender' groups, but each of these comprises two 'races'.[31] While neither of these populations can be superimposed directly on top of the other, they do overlap: in each racial group there are 'women' and 'men', the dominated and the dominant, and in each gender group there are 'whites' and 'blacks', the dominant and the dominated. So, returning to the question of the compatibility of these struggles, we see that the hypothesis holding that the anti-racist and anti-sexist struggles stand in contradiction only makes sense *if we imagine that the people oppressed by racism are all men*; to put it another way, this hypothesis only makes sense on the condition that *the women concerned are not subjected to the racist regime*. Indeed, if this condition were satisfied then racist but anti-sexist measures could indeed be good news for them. However, if we consider these women as

---

31   Since I am not referring to any psychological, cultural or biological reality when I speak of 'race', but rather a social construct, it does not matter if there are *more* than two races, so long as there are *at least* two. No matter how many more there may be, this changes nothing from a theoretical perspective.

part of the racialized group, and thus see them as simultaneously suffering from both racism and sexism, then it is clear that even an anti-sexist measure, as long as it is racist, is a measure against them.

The premises of the dilemma: worthless men and unworthy women

This does not, however, exhaust the terms of the question posed above: for we have not worked through all its underlying premises. After all, by posing this question we do not just imply that the women of the racialized group – women 'from the ghettos' – are oppressed by sexism alone; we also imply that they are only oppressed by *one* sexism: 'their' men's sexism.[32] If they were oppressed by general, ordinary sexism, then why would we bother passing a racist measure? Establishing a balance between the two – anti-sexism *against* anti-racism – implies establishing a balance between the interests of men and women within one same racialized group, and that we think that only by imposing constraints on this group's men will its women's lot be improved. In turn, this implies that this amelioration of their condition will come from targeting *the men of their group, and not men in general.* Thus we will improve these women's lot with a dose of racism, constraining men in a selective manner.

So establishing a balance between anti-sexism and anti-racism means implicitly or unknowingly signing up to the argument according to which the people in these ghettos live in separation from society in general. And as such, not only are the men of this group distinguished by their extraordinary sexism: but the women are also frozen out, and conceptually

---

32   Nacira Guénif-Souilamas, 'De nouveaux ennemis intimes: le garçon arabe et la fille beurette', in Nacira Guénif-Souilamas and Eric Macé, *Les Féministes et le garçon arabe*, Paris: L'Aube, 2004, p. 82.

segregated from society as a whole. It seems that they have nothing to do with other women who don't live in the ghettos; that they are victims of a specific sexism and *only* of this specific sexism.

So the concern for this group of women cannot then be the ordinary concern of one woman for another; rather, it is necessarily a concern from the top down: the concern of the less-oppressed – or 'ordinarily' oppressed – for the more oppressed, or 'extraordinarily' oppressed. But it's also an insulting concern, based on the premise that the women in the ghettos are firstly victims and nothing else; and that they love and live with fathers, brothers, husbands and sons who are not simply sexist like any other men, but are almost *nothing but* sexist. They are entirely defined by their sexism; and in this portrayal there's no space for anything else, or at least anything else positive. These men's unworthiness also casts certain aspersions on the women who love them; what kind of woman would you have to be to love a man like that? So according to the common view (and it's sometimes claimed to be a feminist one) the women of this group should leave these men, who are entirely defined by their negative traits, since you can't expect anything better from them; and in any case, they should stop nurturing any positive feelings in their regard, at the cost of themselves being considered unworthy.[33] Moreover, this is what the group Ni putes ni soumises ['Neither whores nor submissive'] says, and in this it is supported and admired not only by many feminists but also by intellectuals, journalists, politicians and ministers, who give them funding and awards.

---

33   There is no other explanation for the verbal and physical violence perpetrated against women wearing the headscarf: because they refuse to reject their group, and even *flaunt* this stance, they lose the right to the least respect, in particular as concerns their rights.

Whitewashing some or blackening others?

Though Ni putes ni soumises is denouncing a very real sexism – the harassment and violence perpetrated against women is far from imaginary[34] – conversely it seems entirely unaware that sexism and male violence are not exclusive to the ghettos. And a half-truth is a lie. When Samira Belli presented her book *Dans l'enfer des tournantes* ['In the hell of gang rapes'] on TV for the first time, neither the presenter Mireille Dumas nor the other guests mentioned the fact that gang rapes make up just 6 per cent of all recorded rapes (and even this figure doesn't include rapes within the victims' families), nor any of what we knew about gang rapes already: and these are no recent invention in France. This programme succeeded in presenting gang rapes not only as a new phenomenon, but also as one localized within the ghettos: viewers could not have missed the clear implication that this problem comes down to the specific mores of Arab and black rapists.

This unveiling of a terrible reality would have been welcome if it had had the goal of talking about the violence perpetrated against all women in France. But that was not the objective of this TV programme. While Samira Bellil's book was a hit, the media entirely ignored the 2003 ENVEFF report resulting from the first national scholarly study on violence against women. And worse, the report was viciously attacked by academics.[35] So we might well think that the publicity over Bellil's book and the question of 'gang rapes' was not aimed at protecting women as much as stigmatizing boys from the ghettos.[36] The

---

34 Christelle Hamel, '"Faire tourner les Meufs": Les viols collectifs dans les discours des médias et des agresseurs', *Gradiva*, 33, 2003, pp. 85–92.

35 See 'Retournements antiféministes' a report in *Nouvelles Questions féministes*, 22/3, 2003.

36 Christelle Hamel, '"Faire tourner les Meufs"': Les viols collectifs dans les discours des agresseurs et des médias'.

overall effect of this discourse was to produce an image presenting sexism as the sole feat of the men called 'second-generation immigrants' – even though they're French – and telling us that the sexism combatted and defeated in society as a whole ('normal' society) has taken refuge in the ghettos. So now all that's needed to get rid of it entirely is to lay siege to these areas.[37]

The absolution of so-called men of French stock, declared incapable of rape (by omitting any mention of them) had begun. And the selective presentation of sexual violence both laid blame on another group of men *and* exonerated these 'men of French stock' of everything these others were accused of. In this affair it's hard to tell which of these two goals is most consciously sought: whitewashing them, or blackening the others.

Excluding racialized women from women-in-general . . .

This way of looking at these problems and their solution was unable to seduce many of these women of the ghettos. Because it concealed one centrally important fact: *the women of a racialized group are just as much victims of racism as men are.* Certainly, gender oppression does alter racism when the two are combined: racism takes gendered forms, just as gender takes racialized forms. But the fact that the discrimination is different for each gender doesn't mean that it spares either of them.

The 'specific' oppression of women 'of colour' (belonging to racialized or more generally subaltern groups) is one of the major themes of British, Mexican, Indian, Brazilian and North American feminist studies, and it has been the subject of hundreds of works over the last fifteen years.

---

37 And indeed that's what's happening in France at the time of writing.

Even in France – an under-developed country, from this point of view – there are now some works on this theme.[38] But one of the main points made by feminists critical of 'white' feminism[39] is their refusal to consider the different situations of 'Third-World women' (also including Western countries' 'racial minorities', in Chandra Mohanty's work)[40] as *particularisms* with regard to the supposedly 'general' or even 'universal' condition represented by white women.[41] Across the world, feminists belonging to racialized or subaltern groups insist on three points that sometimes make it difficult for them to get along with feminists from the dominant racial groups (namely, 'whites' in Europe and North America, *mestizas* in Mexico, etc). 1) They refuse to separate the feminist struggle from the anti-racist struggle, since sexism and racism indissolubly together constitute their oppression as 'women of colour' (or 'Third-World' or 'racialized' women); 2) they refuse to renounce the objective and subjective solidarities connecting them to the men of their group, who are also racialized; and 3) they challenge any notion that 'their culture' is necessarily more sexist than the dominant group's is, and that they are necessarily 'more oppressed' than the women belonging to this group.

That does not at all mean that they tolerate racialized men's

---

38   In particular see the works by Elsa Dorlin, Elsa Galerand and Jules Falquet, 2005.

39   In her 2005 thesis Sabine Masson provides a very meticulous study of these different feminisms, with the qualifiers 'multiculturalist', 'identity', 'Black' or 'women of colour' (US), 'Black' (UK), 'black' (Brazil), of 'negritude' (Caribbean, Latin America) and finally 'postcolonial (particularly India, US, UK).

40   Chandra Tapalde Mohanty, 'Introduction: Cartographies of struggle', in Chandra Mohanty, Ann Russo and Lourdes Torres, *Third World Women and The Politics of Feminism*, Bloomington: Indiana University Press, 1991.

41   'White' in a sociological sense.

sexism more than any other; but rather, that they cannot ignore what they have in common with these men, any more than they can ignore what they have in common with women from the racially dominant groups. They refuse to apply the strategies for emancipation thought up in different situations as if they were ready-made formulas. They want to wage their struggle on the basis of their own situation of 'double oppression'[42] – of both race and gender – which implies that they are in struggle both with and against the men of their own group as well as both with and against the women of the dominant group.

. . . for the sake of treating them differently . . .

Given the emergence of an *indigène* feminist movement, there's no doubt that we'll soon hear this same critique being expressed in France.[43] But even prior to the women concerned making this explicit, all feminists ought to have been alarmed by the 'solution' that was offered to Arab and black feminists. This solution is nothing new, and was summed up nicely by Ni putes ni soumises spokeswoman Loubna Méliane: the need to 'help women from the ghettos leave their surroundings and their

---

42   We could and should say 'triple oppression', since class plays an important role in this matter. Unfortunately, up to this day it has been the poor relation in this trilogy. We could also debate the term 'double oppression', given its implication of a *quantitatively* double oppression, which is open to question – and has been questioned. Here I use it for simplicity's sake, in order to refer to the multiplicity of systems of oppression.

43   And it already has been – see the programme of the 'women' workshop of the Provence-Côte-d'Azur regional meeting of the Indigènes de la République (5 November 2005): 'How to resist the single model of women's emancipation that today serves as a pretext for discriminatory policies against the most disadvantaged populations. How to articulate women's struggle against patriarchy and the resistance to the ethnic, religious, social and cultural markers imposed by French society. How to build a plural feminism where each woman can find her own path, in accordance with her beliefs.'

families behind'. No less. Did Western feminists in France or Switzerland or Belgium themselves opt for this 'solution'? And did they recommend this same 'solution' to other women, before addressing Arab and black women? They would soon see the extraordinary violence of this supposed 'only solution', if only they took a moment to put themselves in these women's shoes. Women, that is, who they talk about even though they refuse to talk *with them*.[44] We could only dream up such a 'solution', such 'advice', if we were unable to identify with other people's thinking. This advice displays a double standard incompatible with a properly feminist approach: placing greater demands on other women than on yourself or women you consider 'similar' to you. After all, while white feminists and Ni putes ni soumises make this demand on women in ghettos, they would never dream of saying that they themselves – and thus their feminist 'sisters' – need to resort to such a course of action.

Most women, in our society as in others, feel some attachment to their relatives. Feminism denounces the exploitation and violence that takes place in the family not only because these things really happen, but also because this exploitation and violence are all the more scandalous when they take place in what is meant to be a site of affective relations. Even so, no feminist has ever claimed that such attachments are *only* a means of domination – even if they are *also* this – and still less recommended a total breaking-off of all relations. In the here and now, children's attachment to their parents and parents' attachment to their children is very real: we see it every day. In spite of the disagreements and the resentment that they might feel, few children who are not abused will choose to break off all contact with their parents. They prefer to hang on to these ties, even if relationships can be conflict-ridden.

---

44 See Houria Bouteldja, 'On vous a tant aimé-e-s !', *Nouvelles Questions féministes,* 25/1, 2006.

Feminists are no exception to this rule. Why, then, do some of them think that the only solution for women from an 'immigrant background' is to break with their families? Why do they demand something of Arab and black women that would be so painful for them that many prefer to submit to compromise rather than reach such a point? Why do they demand something of these other women that they do not imagine themselves doing? Perhaps because they see these women through a filter of 'otherness', making any empathy or identification with them impossible?

. . . treating them as colonial subjects

For many, the capacity to empathize is the most tried-and-tested of feminist 'techniques'. Feminism starts from the fundamental principle that however varied women's situations may be, they do have one thing in common: patriarchal oppression. Putting this theory into practice requires seeking points of commonality, and thus being able to put yourself in the position of another woman and consider her similar to you: your equal. Arab and black women, who are constantly being told both explicitly and subliminally to leave their families, have every right to be doubly offended. On the one hand, they understand very well the lack of empathy, the inability to identify, and the position of absolute otherness underlying this suggestion; and on the other hand, they resent the image that this proposal gives of them, even if only implicitly. Namely, an image in which their mothers and fathers, sisters and brothers are so worthless that it's unimaginable that they could love them. Not only are their nearest and dearest being called worthless, but so, too, their own feelings for them.

Besides, the 'family' and the 'surroundings' from which we want to 'save' these girls are indeed constraining, like all families and all surroundings, but they are also the site of family and social solidarities that do not exist in the 'outside world'.

And what is meant to be the attraction of this 'outside world': the myth of a non-sexist white man?

We should emphasize the remarkably incoherent presentation of these women in the discourse that the media sets up as the only 'feminist' discourse, whether it emanates from the mouths of women or confirmed male supremacists. They are schoolgirls whom we're going to save from the families who supposedly force them to wear the veil . . . by sending them back to their families; they are the 'others' from the same background as those we claim to be saving them from, who don't ask for this and on the contrary are even more opposed to the bill than the other students.[45] The only point that these varied, often mutually contradictory arguments have in common with their stated objectives resides in a certain outsiders' view of French women of immigrant origin, a view that constructs them as beings who can't tell true from false and good from bad: a population of children who are bound to be 'misled'.[46] Children who we have to decide on behalf of, for their own good. And, moreover, we'll impose this decision by force if necessary. It's no surprise that politicians adopt such an attitude. But how can feminists who denounce men's paternalism not see that the same logic is also at work in the pretence of 'saving' women despite and against their own wishes? How can they not see that violence against children, women and the colonized still employs the

---

45   Patrick Weil, a diehard partisan of the bill, could not even produce one 'of these young Muslim girls who . . . asked for the protection of the law' before the Stasi commission. Patrick Weil, *La République et sa diversité*, Paris: La République des idées, Seuil, 2005. See also Pierre Tevanian, *Le Voile médiatique. Un faux débat: 'l'affaire du foulard islamique'*, p. 80.

46   Suzy Rojtman, Maya Surduts and Josette Trat: 'On ne peut taire les critiques à l'égard du voile au nom de la solidarité avec les jeunes des quartiers populaires. Contre le racisme et pour les femmes', *Libération*, 27 January 2004.

same excuse – the victims' weakness – that paternalism has provided so many times before?[47]

Taking racism seriously: a necessary condition for prosecuting the struggle against patriarchy
One of the measures used to discriminate against a group, other than paternalism, is the constant application of double standards. We demand more of the individuals belonging to the stigmatized group – whether racialized groups, homosexuals or women – than of those who make up the dominant group. They have to 'earn' what others have as a birthright. Enjoining racialized women to leave their families is a good example of this. Certainly we could consider these extra requirements to be based on racism, in that they are addressed to some women and not others; but we could also see them as sexist, since they are not addressed to men of either the dominant or dominated racial group.

Whether pro-ban or still undecided, the feminists who explicitly or implicitly advise the young women of the ghettos to leave their family surroundings are clearly ignorant of these women's attachments and solidarities, built up since childhood. And they need them in order to live, just as us whites do. In so doing, the feminists who mobilized in favour of the law contributed to the construction of an image of the 'world outside the ghetto' as a kind of El Dorado: a place where patriarchy has disappeared. Such an image stands in flat contradiction with the campaigns that these same feminists have run at other times, denouncing the sexism of society 'in general'. It flies in the face of feminism's objectives, which not

---

47   In 'Laïcardes puisque féministes' (*Le Monde*, 29 May 2003) Anne Zélensky and Agnès Roukhline build up the idea that these women's supposed weakness – being 'self-oppressed' – justifies the intervention of legal constraints.

only mean hunting down sexism wherever it exists, but also rejecting the patriarchal idea that it is miraculously absent from certain places and relations – in short, the suggestion that sexism is localized and avoidable.

When they call on the women of the ghettos to leave these spaces, they are implicitly inviting them to find a husband 'of French stock' instead.[48] Well, unless we imagine that the society outside of the ghettos has miraculously become egalitarian, *this means suggesting that they trade in one patriarchy for another.* Without noticing it, here, too – just like the colonists in the Maghreb, and using the same arguments about the *indigènes'* barbarism[49] – they are playing patriarchy's game.

At the heart of the French conception of integration, the injunction for these women to break with their families and surroundings is fundamentally an 'injunction to disloyalty'.[50] Not only does it demand that individuals make an abject disavowal of their nearest and dearest, but it also tends to depersonalize them. If such a project concerned citizens 'of French stock' it would be considered inhuman and even totalitarian. Its desired results would leave the 'children of immigrant parents . . . without a past, without a memory, without history . . . and thus as entirely blank canvasses, easier for others to redesign'.[51] Parents in general naturally see this project as a dangerous one, but it particularly

---

48 Christelle Hamel, 'De la racialisation du sexisme au sexisme identitaire', *Migrations et Sociétés* 17/99–100, May–August 2005, p. 101.

49 Clancy-Smith, 'Le regard colonial: Islam, genre et identités dans la fabrication de l'Algérie française, 1830–1962'.

50 Saïd Bouamama, 'L'ethnicisation des jeunes issus de l'immigration: persistance d'un imaginaire colonial', *Zaama*, proceedings of the conference 'Modes d'émigration et mondes de l'immigration, hommage à Abdelmalek Sayad', December 2005.

51 Sayad, 1994, cited in Saïd Bouamama, 'L'ethnicisation des jeunes issus de l'immigration: persistance d'un imaginaire colonial', p. 64.

troubles the men of the racialized group who live in fear of whites *also* taking 'their' women. This reaction cannot be reduced to some sort of wounded male pride: for a father, 'a so-called "mixed" marriage would mean his daughter validating the stigmatization that targets him as well as all other men considered "Arabs", in presenting him as less desirable than men considered "French"'.[52] But even if we nonetheless considered these fears purely patriarchal, could we as feminists therefore decide that we need not take them into account? Of course not.

If we want to change the world, we can't just ignore it, acting as if it didn't exist. The real world means patriarchy. There is no neutral terrain where we can confront patriarchy in a one-on-one joust in the spirit of fair play. That's just *Ivanhoe*. In real life, we don't choose our battlefield. It's not easy to accept this constraint: we worry that we've lost even before the struggle begins. But this constraint is the condition of all struggles against any kind of oppressive system. Refusing it is simply to evade reality itself; and the cost of that is to renounce any ability to affect it. Everything that minimizes patriarchy or consciousness of its existence flies in the face of feminism, both theoretically and in action. And the same goes for the implicit or explicit argument that patriarchy has disappeared or almost disappeared from society overall: and this is the *necessary premise* of the call on women 'from the ghettos' to leave their own surroundings behind.

But if the claim that patriarchy has disappeared from society as a whole serves as a stepping-stone toward this racist injunction, in turn racism *serves as a stepping-stone toward the anti-feminist argument that patriarchy has disappeared.*

---

52 Christelle Hamel, 'De la racialisation du sexisme au sexisme identitaire', p. 103.

After all, without the support of racist arguments – the opposition between the ghettos on the one hand and 'normal' society on the other – this claim falls apart. The central importance of this opposition is clearly apparent in Élisabeth Badinter's formulation of this argument: 'It [is] unreasonable to put on the same plane the violence against women we see in democratic countries and that which we can see in undemocratic, patriarchal countries. In these latter, violence against women is based on traditionalist, religious and philosophical principles that have nothing to do with our own . . . Conversely, violence against women in our societies runs wholly contrary to our principles . . . above all else it reveals a pathology . . . that requires treatment.'[53]

In this same article, Badinter challenges the results of the ENVEFF study and plays down male violence against women. As we can see, this critique is not based on empirical fact but on an axiom: that violence is 'contrary to our principles'. From this she deduces in a purely rhetorical manner that 'in our country' violence can only be incidental. And the only reason it could be purely incidental in our country is that *patriarchy is located somewhere else.* This assertion of course flies in the face of three decades of feminist activism and research demonstrating the structural character of violence against women. The circularity of this argument is typical – as Leti Volpp tells us[54] – of the discourse of Western superiority in matters of gender. 'The idea that "other" women are subjected to extreme patriarchy is developed in relation to the vision of Western women as secular, liberated, and in total control of their lives. But the assumption that Western women enjoy complete liberation is not grounded in material reality. Rather, Western women's liberation is a

---

53 'La vérité sur les violences conjugales', *L'Express,* 20 June 2005.
54 Leti Volpp, 'Feminism versus Multiculturalism', pp. 1198–9.

product of discursive self-representation, which contrasts Western women's enlightenment with the suffering of the "Third World woman".'[55]

Badinter exoticizes patriarchy and its different forms of violence in order to deny their existence in principle – that is, as a principle of how society functions. She even goes as far as defining certain states as 'patriarchal' – but she only does so in order to be able to assert that other states are not. So we see that orientalism, the exoticization of violence, is the indispensible foundation of this anti-feminist discourse. Similarly, in the commonplace representations of women living in the ghettos – which are so commonplace that they become self-evident 'truths' – we find a revisiting, or even a continuation, of British and French colonial stereotypes of Arabs.[56] And the consequences of this are disastrous. Feminists are still fighting against patriarchy in France, thus affirming that it does indeed exist; yet at the same time, they adopt colonial and orientalist stereotypes that are the stock in trade of the very people they're meant to be fighting against: the camp of patriarchy-deniers,[57] those like

---

55 Ibid.

56 Like the French in the Maghreb, the British in Egypt invoked the veil and 'Islam's treatment of women' as justifications for colonialism. See Leila Ahmed, *Women and Gender in Islam: Historical Roots of a Modern Debate,* Yale: Yale University Press, 1992, p. 152. See also Clancy-Smith, 'Le regard colonial: Islam, genre et identités dans la fabrication de l'Algérie française, 1830–1962'.

57 Need we remind ourselves that this 'denier' camp is also very active in France when it comes to the incestuous sexual violence that men perpetrate against their children (Christine Delphy, 'Retrouver l'élan du féminisme', *Le Monde Diplomatique,* May 2004. Online: http://www.sisyphe.org/imprimer .php3?id_article=1130)? Or that this denial drives a good number of 'perfectly white' women *literally* to flee France for other countries, in the hope of protecting their children? On this same subject, see UN special rapporteur Juan-Miguel Petit's almost wholly ignored report on the situation in France: 'The Special Rapporteur feels that many

Badinter who deny that the oppression of women exists on our shores.

Rethinking the articulation between gender oppression and racial oppression

This last example demonstrates even more forcefully how urgent it is that all feminists, in France as in other countries, think deeply about the links between sexism and racism.

Patriarchy is not the only system that oppresses women from the ghettos. They are also oppressed by racism. These oppressions do not simply follow one after the other, separated in time and space. There is no sign saying 'You're now leaving patriarchy; welcome to racism.' From an individual perspective, these two (or more than two) systems of oppression coexist in the same time and space. They combine. And this combination doesn't resemble either a 'pure' patriarchal oppression or a 'pure' racist one. Do these pure oppressions exist? If a woman *only* suffers from sexism, that means that she otherwise only belongs to the dominant categories of other types of hierarchy like race, nationality, class, age, sexuality, etc. Similarly, if a racialized person *only* suffers from racism, this implies that this person otherwise only belongs to the dominant categories, and in particular, the dominant gender group. In other terms, the prototype victim of racism would be a black man; which is just as absurd as saying

---

individuals in a position of responsibility for the protection of children's rights, particularly within the judiciary, are still largely in denial about the existence and extent of this phenomenon, unable to accept that many of the allegations of sexual abuse may be true and accusing those making the allegations of having a political agenda.' Report submitted by Juan Miguel Petit, Special Rapporteur on the sale of children, child prostitution and child pornography, Addendum, Mission to France, 25–29 November 2002. Available online at http://www.globaldetentionproject.org/fileadmin/docs/2003-report-on-France.pdf.

– following the logic described above – that the prototype victim of sexism is a white woman.

Decentring patriarchy

And often when we speak of the combination of racism and sexism we have in mind a sort of synthesis, which we arrive at by crossing two figures: a *racialized* man and a white *woman*. So in the unconscious representation of the 'essence' of each oppression, its emblematic vision is someone who's privileged in other regards: a victim of racism with gender privilege, or a victim of sexism with white privilege. But why are these situations of relative privilege best-placed to represent each oppression? Why don't we just abandon the idea that some situations are more representative – in short, more *central* – than others? It's not so much that we need to decentre our perspective in order to define patriarchal oppression, as much as we need to *reject the very idea that there is a centre* – to the extent that this centre is identified with *a single* race and class position.

The oppression of racialized women is not a more 'specific' case of racist oppression than racialized men's is; and nor is it a more 'specific' case of patriarchal oppression than white women's. We could term it 'specific' only on condition that we accept that the oppression of white women is also 'specific'; and that being 'non-racialized' or 'white' does not imply some sort of 'absence' from the racist system. The place of the dominant is often mistaken for not being a place at all. Certainly, that is what men are implicitly saying when they suggest that gender is just a matter for women, as do whites when they think that racism only concerns blacks and Arabs. But the reality of the systems of binary hierarchical categorization is that everyone is involved, since there's a place for everyone: for the dominant as well as the dominated.

We urgently need to revisit our way of thinking about the

articulation and imbrication of patriarchy and racism, as well as the way we 'do' activism. The feminist movement cannot survive unless it becomes truly universal, taking all women, all their situations and all their revolts into account. In particular we need to overthrow the premise of Western superiority: for this leads to two different but equally dangerous positions. The first consists of demanding that 'other women' follow strategies developed on the basis of our own position, preventing them from starting out from *their* own situation and freezing them out of feminism if they do not conform to this demand. This just means cutting ourselves off from feminisms 'of colour' or 'Third-World' feminisms. The second proceeds logically from this 'presumption of superiority'[58] to the postulate that the 'other women have drawn the short straw'. In allowing sexism to be localized among certain population groups only – and thus finding 'honorable' reasons to stigmatize them – this postulate itself has two consequences. The first is that certain feminists' participation in the campaign to ban the veil – which had the effect of redoubling the opprobrium already weighing down women and men from colonized backgrounds – placed heavy responsibilities on them as well as all women calling themselves feminists. After all, the great 'liberation of the voice of racism' in the 'debate' over the headscarf made it possible for a national political figure to overtly treat millions of French citizens as potential terrorists,[59] and for police to launch tear gas grenades into a place of worship full of people praying, in Clichy-sous-Bois on 30 October 2005.

The second consequence of this postulate is that in contesting the autochthonous and contemporary character of

---

58   Laura Nader, 'Orientalisme, occidentalisme et contrôle des femmes'.

59   On 16 July 2005, Philippe de Villiers of the right-wing Mouvement Pour la France told TF1 TV news that 'Islam is the breeding ground for Islamism, and Islamism is the breeding ground for terrorism'.

patriarchy in France – and in the West more generally – they denied its extent, its seriousness and even its very existence. Thus Élisabeth Badinter told *L'Arche* magazine: 'This struggle [standing up for women] is aimed at the young women from the first generation of new arrivals, and indeed girls of North African descent. It's for them that we have to fight this battle. *Frankly, for a long time the oppression of women has not existed among people of French stock, whether Jewish or Catholic,*'[60] Since the onset of second-wave feminism, this has been the main argument of all those who want to delegitimize our struggles.

---

60   Élisabeth Badinter (2003), www.col.fr/arche/549- 550/aerr2.htm. Emphasis added.